Kent Dellaire

Billy The Kid
An American Epic Poem

EPICUS Publishing Company
San Francisco, California

Written By: Kent Dellaire
Cover Design: Bruce E. Speed
speedco@mail.com

First Edition
ISBN-13: 978-0-9816132-0-8

Copyright © 2008
EPICUS Publishing Company
San Francisco, California, U.S.A
All Rights Reserved

Printed in the United States of America

CONTENTS

BOOK NUMBER ONE

1. A Riot at Fort Stanton
2. Murphy Builds His Dream House
3. Teetering Towards Bankruptcy
4. An Entrepreneur in Lincoln
5. A Fight Over Life Insurance
6. McSween Up for Embezzlement
7. Dolan Plans Sweet Revenge
8. Brewer in Pursuit of Horses
9. Bonney Splits From the Gang
10. A Long Walk in the Desert
11. Some Fancy Tricks with a Gun
12. Buck Morgan Fires Bonney
13. The Evans Gang Surrenders
14. Tunstall Buys Caseys Cattle
15. Bonney Finds His Lost Horse
16. Dick Brewer Arrests Bonney

CONTENTS
VI

17. A Warrant for McSween's Arrest

18. Why John Chisum Prefers Jail

19. The Cattle King of New Mexico

20. An Outbreak of Small Pox

21. Why Chisum Never Married

22. McSween's Unfair Court Hearing

23. The Events at Shedd's Ranch

24. The First Property Attachment

25. The Second Property Attachment

26. Matthews Gathers the Posse

27. Tunstall Decides to Evacuate

28. Murder on the Road to Lincoln

BOOK NUMBER TWO

29. The Coroner's Inquest Revealed

30. Sheriff Brady Resists Arrest

31. Sebrian Bates Hears a Ghost

32. The Funeral of John Tunstall

CONTENTS
VII

33. They Become the Regulators

34. The Regulators are Arrested

35. The Regulators in Hot Pursuit

36. The Regulators Take Prisoners

37. The Regulators Take Rest

38. The Regulators Take Revenge

39. The Regulators Become Outlaws

40. Jesse Evans Finally Arrested

41. McSween Shows Up at Chisum's

42. An Ambush for Sheriff Brady

43. Deputy Hindmann's Nightmare

44. Bonney Rescues Big Jim French

45. Alex McSween Turns Himself In

46. The Battle with Buckshot Rogers

47. Dick Brewer Dies in the Battle

48. The Trial of Alexander McSween

49. The Decisions of Lincoln County

50. Frank MacNab Dies in Ambush

51. The All Day Long Battle in Town

CONTENTS
VIII

52. MacNab's Murderers Wander Away
53. Murphy Leaves Dolan Everything
54. The Regulators Kill Indian Segovia
55. McSween Recruits a Large Posse
56. The Two Battles of San Patricio
57. A Posse Pursues the Regulators
58. A Fourth of July Celebration
59. Some Barbeque Western Style
60. Bonney's Little Dog Plays Tricks
61. Bonney Helps Martin Chavez

BOOK NUMBER THREE

62. The Five Day Battle Begins
63. The Morning of the First Day
64. The Afternoon of the First Day
65. The Second Day of the Battle
66. The Third Day of the Battle

CONTENTS
IX

67. The Fourth Day of the Battle
68. Around Noon of the Fifth Day
69. Col Dudley Demands Arrests
70. Sue McSween Sees Col Dudley
71. An Interlude in C Sharp Minor
72. A Sudden Evacuation Begins
73. McSween Murdered by Enemies
74. How Some Regulators Escape
75. George Coe's Fabulous Dream
76. Black Fiddler's Dance of Death
77. Three Deputies Come for Salazar
78. McSween's Wife Vows Revenge
79. An Enemy Calls on Sue McSween
80. Bonney Hides From Sheriff Peppin
81. Martinez Kills Morris Bernstein
82. All the Regulators Bid Farewell
83. A Special Agent Reports Corruption
84. Lawyer Chapman Helps McSween
85. Two Rival Gangs Ask for Peace

CONTENTS
X

86. Huston Chapman Dies Like a Hero
87. The Regulators Feel Betrayed
88. Sheriff Kimbrell Looks for Killers
89. Bonney Meets Governor Wallace
90. The Conclusions of the Court - Part I
91. The Conclusions of the Court - Part II
92. The Regulators Free Billy Bonney

BOOK NUMBER FOUR

93. Rob Widenmann Sails to England
94. Lucien Maxwell Buys Fort Sumner
95. Bonney Shoots to Kill Joe Grant
96. The Town Gossips About Bonney
97. Bonney Wants to Kill John Chisum
98. Doc Scurlock Leaves for Texas
99. Pat Garrett Was Elected Sheriff
100. Agents Track Counterfeit Money
101. The Rustlers Steal Some Groceries

CONTENTS
XI

102. The Rustlers Flee from Ambush
103. The Rustlers Kill Deputy Carlyle
104. Pat Garrett Pursues the Rustlers
105. Pat Garrett Takes Prisoners to Jail
106. Pat Garrett Resists Deputy Leyba
107. Stewart Enlists Texas Cowboys
108. Pat Garrett Sets the Death Trap
109. Pat Garrett Shoots Tom O'Folliard
110. O'Folliard Dies from His Wounds
111. Pat Garrett Follows a Cold Trail
112. Pat Garrett Kills Charlie Bowdre
113. Capture at Stinking Springs - Part I
114. Capture at Stinking Springs - Part II
115. The New Celebrities of Las Vegas
116. An Angry Mob Stops the Train
117. The Court Reopens in the Spring
118. Bonney Was Sentenced to Hang
119. Bonney Was Escorted to Lincoln
120. Bob Olinger Tries to Bully Bonney

CONTENTS
XII

121. Bonney Recalls Stepfather Antrim
122. Kid Antrim Shoots Windy Cahill
123. Billy the Kid Shoots James W. Bell
124. Billy the Kid Shoots Bob Olinger
125. Billy the Kid Makes His Escape
126. Pat Garrett Hurries for Lincoln
127. Billy the Kid Heads for Fort Sumner
128. Billy the Kid Meets Abrana Garcia
129. Billy the Kid's Last Day at Home
130. Billy the Kid's Unfinished Business
131. John Poe Arrives on the Scene
132. Garrett Kills Billy the Kid - Part I
133. Garrett Kills Billy the Kid - Part II

APPENDIX
152
153

BIBLIOGRAPHY
154

PREFACE
XIII

As every reader will quickly discover, I have used no punctuation other than apostrophes in writing this epic poem. I allowed myself this one luxury. However, I only used an apostrophe if I found that it helped me to more easily complete a line of verse. If this was not the case, then I did not use it. (I did use one hyphen, but who's counting?) Punctuation can be seen as a fairly new invention, since neither the ancient Romans nor the Greeks used it. What I have done instead is to use space around each verse, which basically serves the same purpose, since it helps the reader to pause when necessary.

Since our modern world has only rare examples of epic poems, I have looked to the Renaissance for inspiration, hoping to give rebirth to this once noble art form. Therefore, it will be up to the reader to judge, as to how far I have succeeded or failed. Originality is always hard to achieve. But I have done so in justifying a page, naturally. By that I mean using a word with the exact length needed to complete a line of verse, so that all of the verses line up evenly on the right side of the page. I like to think of this as a kind of mosaic, where different size words fit into place to make an image, in this case a word picture. I doubt if this could be done without computers, since they allow for fast editing. To me, the benefit of this outweighs the difficulty, since close rhythmic patterns are developed, that help to further the drama of the story. Also, the absence of punctuation lets the epic poem flow, like it was written in one continuous sentence. The result, when at its best, allows the words to cascade down the page, like a waterfall.

In addition, each page tells an episode within the story, which I further divided into four books, since the story seemed to have natural breaks there. Hoping to preserve accuracy, I used the best historical sources and documents that were available to me. There are one hundred and thirty three pages, which may be read separately or all together. It may be easier to think of the pages as a kind of sophisticated word play, like cross word puzzles, etc. I have carefully constructed them to read like a modern story. In fact, if heard with the eyes closed, most people would only hear a slight difference, in particular the end rhymes. I sincerely hope that you will enjoy reading this epic poem.

Kent Dellaire

BOOK ONE

A Riot at Fort Stanton
1

Everyone at Ft Stanton knew the brains
Behind the store could only be Colonel
Emil Fritz a German officer who trains
All the young clerks who have funneled

Through the store over his long tenure
And whose idea it was to set the still
For corn whiskey by burning the manure
From buffalos and which requires skill

To brew and transport undetected under
The noses of guards who patrol through
The area searching for illegal plunder
A plan that worked until several rough

Soldiers decided to drink with Indians
During the celebration of Independence
And then got so drunk that the Indians
Hopped about whooping and took offence

When soldiers had caught them stealing
Horses that caused a riot to break out
At the fort where everyone was reeling
From the whiskey and heard Fritz shout

He would not be responsible as long as
The officer who was in charge insisted
They had been swindled by a horses ass
Then insulted the officer who resisted

Arrest by the guards who got called in
To establish calm that resembled order
All around that fort the next day when
A commander Dudley appointed a soldier

To investigate additional charges that
Folks were being swindled by the store
Because of exorbitant prices for a hat
Or for about anything you bought there

For that matter making Lawrence Murphy
Resign a commission from the army when
Emil Fritz in moods that sounded huffy
Said he was going back to Germany then

Because he had terminal kidney disease
And wanted to visit Deutschland before
He succumbed to death hoping new peace
Filled up his heart and soul once more

Murphy Builds His Dream House
2

What would Lawrence Murphy do now that
Fritz his partner had left for Germany
Most folks in town would eat their hat
To know the answer which not very many

Had guessed right since they just knew
Only small parts of a picture although
Some claimed Lawrence Murphy was a new
Man soon after he saw partner Fritz go

On a train back to New York on account
He stayed drunk in his room for a week
After he came back then began to mount
His horse and then ride hoping to seek

Advice of James Dolan a junior partner
In the post store who cared for Murphy
And substituted him for his own father
Since they shared a similar philosophy

Which was to get rich soon as possible
And some said this was the real reason
Why Lawrence Murphy did the improbable
When he took a loan from Thomas Catron

The Officer of the First National Bank
To build from scratch a huge two story
Mercantile store not far from the bank
Of Benito River and so bathed in glory

Soon after he returned to Lincoln from
Santa Fe and began construction on the
House which he later stocked with some
Mercantile tools and dry goods that he

Got on credit with the same company as
Before called the Spiegelberg Brothers
And almost instantly discovered it was
Hard to pay for weekly bills as others

Had predicted it would be and so began
To almost at once look around for ways
That would create lots more money than
What the store could make in some days

Which was nothing so after awhile some
Began to talk about Murphy and say how
Folks went unpaid because of no income
Ever since the house became a pink cow

Teetering Towards Bankruptcy
3

It was then that another tall Irishman
John Riley would rescue Murphy's store
When Dolan an extraordinary little man
Irish too and hardly four feet or more

Who was once a drummer boy in the army
Asked him to be a partner in the House
Because his cattle amounted to so many
Around eight thousand some would guess

May be higher but nobody knew for sure
Just how many since the amount changed
Because gangs of rustlers would insure
The level of numbers could be arranged

When Riley had won army beef contracts
To regularly supply that Indian Agency
Whose job was to feed tribes on tracts
Of land called Reservations an urgency

That existed since the buffalos hunted
By white men were driven to extinction
A fact of unconcern when Riley grunted
An aside to Dolan a man of distinction

That he found ways to increase profits
By telling the army more Indians lived
On reservations than soldiers had wits
To accurately count since few survived

Diseases white men brought from Europe
Like small pox and so took any comfort
They could find in little ways to cope
With loses and that was drinking a lot

Of fire water another name for whiskey
Smuggled into them by Murphy and Dolan
Who once suggested that the whole army
Should look for missing Braves on land

Outside the agency to increase numbers
And translate this into more beef sold
On account of many thieves and robbers
Are raiding ranches while growing bold

And drunk on whiskey made of corn mash
The Indians planted and grew then sold
To traders who then traded it for cash
In barters as old as the hills are old

An Entrepreneur in Lincoln

John Tunstall from England was wealthy
And came to New Mexico for two reasons
First the sun and dry air were healthy
And second John wanted to find persons

Who can help him reach his lifes goals
Which were to build a big cattle ranch
While navigating through narrow shoals
And jagged rocky bottoms that can much

Havoc do to ships that sail on unaware
Of the dangers and secondly to operate
A large store stocked up with hardware
But unlike Murphys seen as second rate

Which was why he was glad when McSween
Whom he met while in Santa Fe had told
Him as soon as he arrived on the scene
That Murphy and Dolan had not yet sold

Fairview Ranch a sale which he advised
Tunstall to stay away from since Dolan
Had talked about the deal and promised
To award him as part of a devious plan

Five thousand dollars if he could talk
Him Tunstall into buying it to relieve
Murphy of a big burden so he will walk
Away from all debt and this on the eve

When they become partners in the store
Dolan and Riley who also become rivals
When he decides to build his own store
Which the ripeness of time now reveals

This good sound advice from the lawyer
Who suggested that the Desert Land Act
Of New Mexico had provided every buyer
The opportunity to claim a large tract

Of land amounting to hundreds of acres
With only this one catch that the land
Be worked and improved for three years
Until an oasis blooms from desert sand

When waters in irrigation ditches flow
From the Rio Feliz and sprout greenery
Where row on row of healthy crops grow
That when harvested overflow a granary

The Fight Over Life Insurance

Then one day they heard Fritz had died
Leaving behind a life insurance policy
Worth ten thousand dollars for kindred
At Lincoln a steak so tender and juicy

Murphy and Dolan in order to get hands
On a piece took his relatives to court
So everybody in the county understands
Fritz left behind debts and owed a lot

Of money around forty thousand dollars
To their store but when months pass by
Still without payments these two liars
Hire a lawyer Alexander McSween to try

And untangle that legal knot around it
Which necessitates that he travel east
To New York City the capitol of profit
And loss in America where at long last

He solves the problem inside an office
Of the Spiegelberg Brothers who settle
On Fritzs old debts for the fair price
Of seven hundred wishing not to mettle

Further with the account since McSween
Paid them in cash with a loan promised
By Dunnel and Lawson Bank a go between
That released a policy but compromised

The situation since interest penalties
Had to be paid from the total benefits
So all of this Alexander McSween tries
To tell Murphy and Dolan who have fits

About it but were glad that the matter
Was over after his return on the train
That crisscrossed a country now fatter
Than ever since there was much to gain

McSween destined to profit on the deal
After the firm in New York transferred
Money to his account so none may steal
Of the proceeds until he has conferred

With a court in Lincoln and will learn
The decisions made by a judge who sits
On the bench and says his only concern
The store claimed too much in benefits

McSween Up for Embezzlement

Soon McSween requested and was granted
By the court permission to do an audit
On the Houses ledgers that had slanted
The amount of Fritzs debt for a profit

Since the real debt was three thousand
A whole forty thousand less than asked
By Dolan and Murphy who really planned
To pay on their mortgage having risked

Their reputations with the townspeople
By hoping their lies went undiscovered
Since illegal news would send a ripple
Like drops in still water that wavered

On the surface an event they must stop
If they could and so they paid a visit
To the Fritz Ranch where they now hope
Emils relatives will sign an affidavit

That charges McSween with embezzlement
For withholding back on life insurance
Until this pair arrive at a settlement
That gave brother and sister assurance

They shall receive half of what is due
And then proceed on to lawyer Rynerson
Who prosecutes the case without a clue
For what's gone on before this session

Proof that lawyers set aside the truth
When more profit can be made from lies
Something after all that was okay with
Lawyer McSween who sat and never tries

To win the settlement outside of court
Knowing from past experience the House
Pays its bills but only as last resort
And so wants a jury who has more horse

Sense than all his current adversaries
Put together because he believes Dolan
Would fail to pay in full his salaries
And for all of his travel expenses and

For his nightly lodging and plus meals
And incidentals each good company pays
For its employee without cutting deals
Of any kind no matter what anyone says

Dolan Plans Sweet Revenge

McSween and Tunstall were not partners
But Dolan had lately become suspicious
Of them after he watched their manners
Together and so Dolan was very jealous

And by nature he had become a thorough
Man who liked a swift course of action
Having learned over the years of rough
drill in the army how to pay attention

To details and doing this out of habit
He became one of the closes confidants
To Judge Bristol who would have to sit
Uncomfortably to hear one of his rants

That cleverly grasped this opportunity
And demanded Sheriff Bradys attachment
Should not exclude Tunstall's property
Or McSween's from any final settlement

Or ruling the court made during future
Transactions because of life insurance
Proceeds whose existence seemed unsure
And to all this Bristol agreed at once

But Dolan liked more immediate results
Since the court was not due to convene
For weeks and adding injury to insults
Dolan hired men to act as a go between

Since he himself would never take part
Directly in a crime of stealing horses
From Tunstalls ranch he liking the art
Of delegation and soon a plan endorses

By sending Jesse Evans and his gang of
Outlaws who Dolan knew from Ft Stanton
In the days when they found his office
Handy after cattle drives they were on

Had delivered beef to the fort that by
The way was not a traditional stockade
But clusters of houses open to the sky
With large grounds for military parade

Barracked with Negroes who the Indians
Named Buffalo Soldiers for their curly
Black hairs along with their civilians
To whom Dolan acted superior and surly

Brewer in Pursuit of Horses

When Tunstall learned from his foreman
Dick Brewer that a gang had stolen all
Of his horses they come up with a plan
And then almost immediately pay a call

On Charlie Bowdre and Dr Scurlock some
Of their closest neighbors who of late
Call the Ruidoso Valley their new home
And who will help them since they hate

To see a mans horses robbed by thieves
Who in no time at all they shall track
To Shedd's Ranch where Brewer believes
They may be hiding and soon comes back

From La Cruces disappointed at Sheriff
Barela who said he was busy with other
Things and treated the situation as if
Of no consequence he hoping to smother

The spark leading to the investigation
That Brewer realized they must achieve
Without arrest warrants an indignation
That no apology of Barelas can relieve

Since they must ride after the thieves
All alone then search around for Jesse
Who soon appears under the porch eaves
At seeing them then grins at the posse

Who Brewer has stopped near the corral
Noticing their horses and then demands
That they be returned but loses morale
Instantly after he sees Jesse commands

A dozen cowboys who armed with pistols
Stand haphazardly up against the porch
And everyone of them are Murphys tools
Including Billy Bonney who will crouch

On his heels sucking at the long straw
In his mouth saying nothing when Evans
Joked he wasn't such a terrible outlaw
Telling Dick he can with his own hands

Retrieve his horse but that the horses
In the corral stayed so Brewer flushed
In anger then rode away with his posse
That pride feeling temporarily crushed

Bonney Splits From the Gang

Then the Jesse Evans Gang would alight
At a hideaway in the forested mountain
Where they were visited late one night
By John Riley who arrived to ascertain

Whether or not they could steal cattle
From Chisum to restock their own herds
Whose number slowly dwindled to little
More than several thousand these words

Spoken just before Billy Bonney walked
In the door to join the others who sat
Near the stove to keep warm and talked
Quietly together no one removing a hat

From the top of his head when suddenly
Riley became mad at Bonney who he said
Had stolen a horse and quite foolishly
From Sheriff Barelas daughter who paid

A fortune for it and wanted her father
To arrest the outlaw who had stolen it
Who would be you Riley repeated rather
Loudly to Bonney he not caring one bit

Who overheard the conversation so long
As Bonney agreed to give the mare back
No later than tomorrow because a wrong
Move like that can leave an easy track

For Barela to discover their operation
So Bonney shrugged and though mumbling
Offered to give Riley full cooperation
Before he went out that door stumbling

Into Tom O'Keefe who Bonney made known
What happened and knowing that O'Keefe
Was someone whose discontent had grown
Bonney searches for food however brief

In the cooks stores so the two friends
Can slip out unnoticed before the dawn
When a bright golden sunlight descends
In the room an hour before others yawn

And rise to find Billy has ridden away
On the little mare of incredible speed
And stamina that there was just no way
They can catch him on his stolen steed

A Long Walk in the Desert

The gang split up and rode three ways
After stealing John Tunstall's horses
Which include two fine carriage grays
That was when the two boys met forces

They couldn't resist - Apache Indians
Who had wandered from the reservation
To run them off their sacred mountain
Where tribes were dying of starvation

From hunters who killed their animals
And rustlers too who stole the cattle
An unfortunate situation that appalls
And likewise shakes a medicine rattle

Four reasons why warriors held rifles
Looked for tracks and beat the bushes
Next to where a hand silently stifles
A cough and tenses while a man pushes

Near enough to spit on but runs after
The fleeing mare with an empty saddle
So he must wander in the desert later
With a canteen holding a water puddle

That after three days has a few drops
Left in it on account of sun and sand
So that parched lips express no hopes
For Tom O'Keefe when some Indian band

Pursued him and he vanished with them
On the horizon and left him all alone
With the harvest moon and the problem
Of how to survive like a living stone

Which somehow or the other did happen
He showed in one piece at Jones ranch
And it was Barbara who looked up when
He passed right under the tree branch

And then came in thru the screen door
Of the porch and asked for some water
When she hurried up to dress his sore
Burns with hog grease and still later

Gave him steak to eat and a clean bed
Where he slept that night and most of
The next day until his old weary head
Felt normal again because of her love

Some Fancy Tricks with a Gun

Yes her love that cared for his wounds
And cooked breakfast for him with eggs
Taken from the coop next to the hounds
Until he was able to stand on his legs

And ride the horse that she loaned him
So he could work the cattle once again
For the Dolan Ranch where he left them
One morning then rode across the plain

With her son John Jones who would look
For a job there too and was having fun
Watching Billy undo his scabbards hook
And try some fancy tricks with his gun

Like when he spun a pistol in his hand
So that it revolved like a child's toy
As it went around his index finger and
Was positively amazing stuff for a boy

Who was almost a man not yet seventeen
But that was not anywhere near as good
As the second trick when he would lean
Out of the saddle and aim for the wood

While the chestnut went at full gallop
Then instantly shoot the first sparrow
From the branch just when it would hop
And this followed by two more in a row

In flight one far off the other closer
All with the same care and precise eye
And hand movement working all together
Well enough so that John uttered a cry

Of unbelief and then ran to the bushes
Looking for the three birds that Billy
Assured him he killed and then blushes
While he found only two birds that lay

In the tumble weeds with feathers gone
So that the Kid would point just where
Exactly in the field was the third one
And John would run and bend over there

And pick it up with his curled fingers
Then throw it back down after the game
Was over and just like one who lingers
Inform Billy that he felt put to shame

Buck Morgan Fires Bonney

When they rode through the arched gate
That led up to Murphy's Fairview Ranch
Buck Morgan the foreman who would hate
Bonney for kissing a senorita at lunch

Whom Buck loved and now couldn't trust
Dashed over to tell Billy he was fired
For leaving branding irons out to rust
In the rain where the cattle got mired

About knee deep in mud and where ropes
Were thrown to put a well placed lasso
Over the long horns of steers in hopes
That cowboys could make everyone to go

On its own power without need of force
Because the ground was like quick sand
At a time a cowboy relied on his horse
With only a pressure from his knee and

The horse quickly jumped left or right
Depending on the direction steers took
Since herds bolt from flashes of light
From the sounds of thunder which shook

The ground and then started a stampede
In the herds which every cowboy risked
Breaking a bone maybe a neck to impede
The progress of the herd or be whisked

Away by the seething mass which is why
Bonney couldn't understand Buck Morgan
And since he was not one for being shy
Billy told Buck he sucked a male organ

And called him a rotten son of a bitch
For firing a man for something trivial
And so then Bucks face began to twitch
From nerves at staring down this rival

Who was only a young boy and yet dared
Question his authority even unto death
And so for a moment the two men stared
Until Morgan sighed and exhaled breath

By telling Bonney to leave this second
Before he shouted to the boys for help
And Bonney did too because he reckoned
He could wait awhile for Morgans scalp

The Evans Gang Surrenders
13

No sooner had Justice Wilson made Dick
Brewer a constable than a posse formed
With the purpose to find and then lick
Jesse Evans whole gang that had roamed

Hereabout stealing mostly and was last
Spotted holding up at Beckwith's Ranch
A name which Sheriff Brady in the past
Had frequently gone to visit for lunch

And been on friendly terms and so that
Was the reason why Sheriff Brady tried
To stall the men as he leaned and spat
Tobacco juice upon the ground and lied

When he told them he was sure the gang
Wasn't within fifty miles and then had
To eat his words afterward when a bang
From a rifle revealed they were inside

But after negotiations said they would
Surrender and soon did with their arms
Above their heads when they understood
The Sheriff would keep them from harms

Way when they took the road to Lincoln
Where just by coincidence they meet up
With Tunstall driving his supply wagon
Headed for Chisums who soon shall stop

To thank everybody for a job well done
And then ask Jesse Evans what they did
With those horses that they had stolen
While in the presence of Billy the Kid

Since Evans would tell him for whiskey
He said and after gave a sheepish grin
To Tom hill and even if this was risky
Tunstall agreed if only somehow to win

Over that Jesse Evans gang to his side
But after a drink try hard as he could
He didn't recall anything and had lied
Telling him two of his mules were sold

To a small humble priest in New Mexico
Who claimed a poor old mother had died
After which Tunstall would suddenly go
Hoping none of them would see he cried

Tunstall Buys Caseys Cattle
14

The idea was McSween's who first heard
From the Spiegelberg brothers directly
When they hired him to attach the herd
Of four hundred cattle toward security

Against the debt run up by Ellen Casey
Which he did do with help from Sheriff
Brady who won a second election easily
Then cautioned Ellen she would lose if

These brothers know she can't pay them
The money she owed which everyone knew
She didn't have and solved the problem
Of acquiring the herd and starting new

In the ranch business with two hundred
And nine beeves not much when compared
To Chisums vast herd but Brewer stored
Ellens at his ranch where no one cared

Two cents what Mrs Casey thought about
All of this until she claimed Tunstall
Had stolen her cattle making her shout
Orders for her boys to retake them all

Which they did and then drove to Texas
Hoping to sell them for a higher price
Since she didn't earn enough for taxes
When stopped by Brewer who wasn't nice

When he called the lady a bigger thief
Than Jesse Evans Gang and then held up
The wagon not so as to give more grief
But grant his boys time in the stirrup

While they chased the cows in the lead
Shooting guns in a very short distance
Turning back the herd so they can head
For Glenco when Mrs Casey would glance

Up at Dick Brewer her eyes opened wide
Believing he might try capture her two
Grown boys or shoot them from the side
While the Brewer posse rode on through

Chaparral the reason for leather chaps
On the legs before Mrs Casey dared say
Anything then said I was wrong perhaps
Don't shoot my boys not my boys I pray

Bonney Finds His Lost Horse
15

Billy Bonney liked nothing better than
A very fast horse and so when he heard
The same horse he'd lost in the Indian
Attack was moving to Texas with a herd

Stolen by ranch widow Mrs Robert Casey
Bonney rode with Brewers posse at once
Thinking this was extraordinarily easy
A job that can be preformed by a dunce

And so when that posse had almost gone
Bonney with hat in hand told the widow
Her cattle horse was stolen by someone
To which Casey said I'll have you know

I bought it from a respectable rancher
And still have the bill of sale for it
Until realizing he had to convince her
He said Ma'am I don't doubt that a bit

But I really should know seeing as how
My friend and me took it during a race
He won but left before taking any bows
And then met me at a prearranged place

Where I got the horse and he the purse
A wild story that threw the poor widow
For a big loop so that she would curse
Billy who said it didn't matter anyhow

To him for all he cared she could keep
The horse as long as he could go along
With them to Texas causing her to leap
In the saddle and then like a longhorn

Want to gouge out both of his big eyes
Using her fingers but didn't of course
Then she not wanting to hear more lies
Said leave her be and struck her horse

With spurs and quickly dashed on ahead
Of the wagon and Bonney watched her go
The horse running as the wind and said
Turning to forgotten friend George Coe

That is a fine looking animal bringing
This response from him why Ellen Casey
Sure was that all right until laughing
George ran after a disappointed Bonney

Dick Brewer Arrests Bonney

One time Bonney stayed with George Coe
On a small ranch in the Ruidoso Valley
Where they hunted deer in ice and snow
Ate venison and became satisfied fully

Near fires of the cast iron wood stove
Where even into spring they talked for
Hours until one day Brewer would shove
A gun at Bonney when he opens the door

Then arrests him for being in the gang
With Jesse Evans who stole many horses
From John Tunstall because a bird sang
Into Brewer's ear and further stresses

The fact he would be locked up in jail
With the gang who was about dead drunk
As they arrived in town since Tunstall
Had brought whiskey so much they stunk

From lying in their own puke but awoke
To welcome Bonney who Brewer took away
So he could talk to Tunstall who spoke
To tell Bonney he did not have to stay

But he could be released when he chose
By coming to work for him on his ranch
A proposal from which he couldn't lose
Since he would only trade a wild bunch

For something better which he accepted
In less time than it took to don a hat
Knowing full well he would be expected
To appear in court as a matter of fact

When he knew he would have less memory
Over exact details about what happened
Than he did now when he told the story
To that court judge and so this opened

A new page in the life of Billy Bonney
Who quickly came to respect and admire
Tunstall's ability for acquiring money
And business sense setting him on fire

To learn something different every day
From books in a library McSween loaned
Him as he listened to Sue McSween play
The towns one and only piano she owned

A Warrant for McSweens Arrest

Then one day in early January eighteen
Hundred and seventy eight the overland
Stage carried lawyer Alexander McSween
Along with his wife Sue and old friend

John Chisum the biggest cattle rancher
In New Mexico to the town of Las Vegas
Where a most strange event would occur
In that the group could no longer pass

On through since warrants were pending
Because Alex McSween was being charged
For embezzlement in some condescending
Plot and yet because the lawyer argued

Their basic legal rights were violated
Since Sheriff Romero could not produce
His warrant or Chisums on an unrelated
Issue Sheriff Romero turned them loose

So they could freely ride on the stage
And leave under a clouded circumstance
So troubled Attorney Catron would rage
After reading a message just by chance

That had come over the telegraph wires
In Santa Fe saying Jim Dolan persuaded
Fritzs relatives this lawyer conspires
To keep the proud family name degraded

By absconding with the insurance money
While McSween believed the accusations
On the other hand were strangely funny
And in retrospect more weird gyrations

In the treatment he now fully expected
From James Dolans unpredictable temper
When suddenly on a knoll they detected
Over the deep purple sage a lone rider

Who appeared with telegraphed warrants
For Sheriff Romero who stopped at once
And threw John Chisum out on his pants
As two Deputies accompanied by a dunce

Arrested the two men but let the woman
Go on that stage destined for St Louis
Prompting her to remark this was a man
A Sheriff who she didn't dare to trust

Why John Chisum Prefers Jail

These were the reasons why James Dolan
Was jealous of the McSweens because he
Erected a fine new house right in town
Costing more money than any lawyer fee

That Dolan paid him and must therefore
Used insurance funds to pay for it all
Since he became a resident just before
That friend of his named John Tunstall

Moved in to build a store that rivaled
His own store seated across the street
Where every man and woman now marveled
At that new bank where they could meet

Inside to secure low interest payments
From the three officers namely McSween
Tunstall and Chisum who often comments
He felt as if he was caught in between

Opposing groups engaged in tugs of war
When he left on the stage for St Louis
And he was accused of breaking the law
Then caught and arrested on some bogus

Charge of giving out notes in exchange
For cattle that were never his to sell
In the first place a charge so strange
Honest John Chisum must say go to hell

He would rather spend his time in jail
Than tell the courts how much his land
Was worth counting every last cow tail
Since the law was like a tyrant's hand

So much so that when Alexander McSween
Left in the company of Sheriff Barrier
And Antonio Campos who he rode between
Chisum would write and send by carrier

Detailed letters which his niece Sally
Wanted to include one day in her diary
Because Uncle John was innocent really
And his arrest had been so unnecessary

Because unscrupulous lawyers had filed
False accusations to gain his property
So John took four days of being jailed
Rather than bend to criminal authority

The Cattle King of New Mexico
19

Cattle roamed three hundred miles over
Bosque Grande Ranch through open range
Around eighteen miles from Fort Sumner
Where nobody at all thought it strange

To see rustlers making off with dozens
Of steers which would wind up in Texas
Or perhaps even the agency for Indians
Till one day having had enough at last

John Chisum stormed the Beckwith place
With his cowboys who began to shoot it
Out with thieves whom they would chase
Inside after catching this same outfit

Red handed changing his Longrail brand
To the single arrow of Lawrence Murphy
Who without any shame takes this stand
It being part of his cosmic philosophy

To work with the Seven Rivers Warriors
Then much later with Jesse Evan's gang
Who learned with and would take orders
From John Kinney when the bullets sang

In the air over their heads after what
Eventually became a stand off for both
Sides so much so that Chisum called it
Quits and then went home but was loath

To stop here and so followed the trail
Of fresh cattle prints that would lead
To El Paso where he soon sees the rail
That was his brand and with good speed

Recovered many cattle that were stolen
Until one bad incident gave him fright
When he searched a poor shack and then
Suddenly witnessed this terrible sight

Several children who were lying in bed
Their malnourished bodies deathly sick
Showing small pox scabs upon each head
The runny pustules having turned black

And infected as the steer was hog tied
With a rope just under a high bunk bed
Which he untied and soon the steer led
Outside feeling uneasy now and worried

An Out Break of Small Pox

Within a few days Chisum left El Paso
Driving before him the herd of cattle
Which he journeyed with to New Mexico
Putting many long hours in the saddle

To join his outfit near the mountains
The Guadalupe and stream the Delaware
When he began to have aches and pains
Blaming them on his long trip unaware

That he now had small pox the disease
That others diagnosed since they knew
The symptoms and urged a time of ease
Which for John a restless man was new

Because he liked overseeing the drive
During the spring as cowboys round up
The calves born on the range and give
Each one a hot iron brand on the rump

But Chisum took their advice and went
To lay on his cot with a rising fever
While Frank a one time slave was sent
To Fort Stanton a trip he would cover

In four days riding all night and day
Only stopping to rest his tired horse
At Ft Stanton before going on his way
Carrying medications to save his boss

Who to his great surprise got soaking
Wet when the water flooded the stream
Because of rain then continued rising
Around his cot like in some bad dream

Until nurses moved him to a dry place
After water had soothed his condition
Seemingly unbearable leaving his face
With the pitted and marked complexion

That would fade in time after he rode
Back to Bosque where he would recover
In his home which would later explode
When Buck Powell came with a revolver

To arrest him for attacking Beckwiths
Ranch and about jumped from his socks
When he learned Chisum came down with
Sickness and left not wanting the pox

Why Chisum Never Married

As it just so happens John Chisum told
Miss Lily Casey the reasons why he can
Never marry in his life but would stay
A bachelor even while Chisum was a man

Considered a good catch for most women
Who sew home sweet home but not always
Especially earlier on when he was then
A lot poorer and lacked means and ways

To support a family even though he and
Sue Holman would talk about the future
Together as if John asked for her hand
In marriage already and they felt sure

They would tie the knot something that
Mr Cheatham his employer wanted to see
Before that city dude with a fancy hat
Becomes the reason why Sue became free

For one year even after John had asked
Her to marry now that he was a partner
In the store and then foolishly risked
This relationship because he loved her

And would from pride demand they marry
Right after she made her wedding dress
And Sue made a decision she felt sorry
About after enduring a lot of distress

Because she married that city dude out
Of spite then survived in dire poverty
In California because the witless lout
Did not have a job or his own property

Or things a pretty young woman who was
The school's class belle should expect
In life and would have had too because
John Chisum had acquired great respect

For his business when he became richer
Than other men and could easily afford
Sue Holman who yesterday said from her
Mouth she had loved him well dear Lord

Just think of the irony involved in it
When he told Lilly who accompanied him
In his buggy he felt so blue in spirit
He drank a brandy bubbling at the brim

McSweens Unfair Court Hearing
22

When McSween and party reached Lincoln
On the way to La Mesilla they got word
Judge Bristol was ill and so stayed on
Without Mr Campos who could not afford

To waste time so returned to Las Vegas
While Deputy Barrier put McSween under
House arrest until it was time at last
To discover that with a kind of wonder

McSweens hearing would not be at court
But within that house of Judge Bristol
Who could not be moved because of gout
And for his own security kept a pistol

Inside of his desk from where he heard
William Rynerson carry the prosecution
Speaking caustically in his long beard
Just as if though asking for execution

Of the defendant whenever Alex McSween
Explained reasons why his bank account
Still had Fritz's insurance money when
Emily and Charles Fritz on every count

Had refused to accept a generous offer
Of delivering their share of the money
After he deducted typical expenses for
The rent of rooms and the long journey

By steam trains to New York City where
He had to dicker with frontier traders
The Spiegelberg Brothers to earn their
Release of any claims all like ladders

Of firemen he must climb before coming
To the roofs and if that wasn't enough
McSween said his reason for them going
To St Louis was to buy necessary stuff

For his brand new house like furniture
No one manufactured in Lincoln and not
To run away as stated since his future
Was there an idea that Rynerson fought

Loud and long enough so that the judge
Set McSween's trial during an argument
From which neither man wanted to budge
When Bristol read aloud the indictment

The Events at Shedds Ranch

Shedds Ranch was between the two towns
La Mesilla and Lincoln where everybody
Stopped to refresh the horses and cows
With water and feed and meet an oddity

Of people on beaten paths to the store
And saloon and where anyone with money
Could rent a room or bunk on the floor
As did McSween and Tunstall and Bonney

Who saw Jesse Evans there and Tom Hill
And Frank Baker and others in the band
Who were no longer sitting in the jail
Because Dolan found money for the bond

And it was there that Jesse Evans told
Bonney Sheriff Barela would arrest him
Since it mattered not who finally sold
His daughters horse to Casey on a whim

Even though Bonney had tried to return
The mare and failed when suddenly both
Heard a ruckus outside and would learn
Instantly that Dolan was being uncouth

In his description of Tunstall and saw
Just then how the two adversaries were
Like fighting cocks about to go to war
Battle each other right then and there

Before Deputy Barrier stood in between
To hurriedly usher John Tunstall aside
Telling him that he had to get McSween
Safely to Lincoln then saved his pride

His ruffled feathers since their party
Left earlier than many others to avoid
More trouble for Tunstall whose hearty
Disposition crumbled as McSween buoyed

Them up with reason in which he always
Found refuge when embroiled by emotion
Which can lead to mankinds darker ways
When all at once there was a commotion

As the Jesse Evans gang rushed on past
Making everyone wonder what this meant
Since the gang deserved their distrust
By taking Sheriff Brady the attachment

The First Property Attachment

McSween knew in advance that the court
Would attach all of his property since
He refused to give up his bank account
Which held less than ten thousand once

They had arrived in Lincoln but no one
Bothered to say the court would attach
John Tunstall's property till later on
When they came to town and would catch

Sheriff Brady and his men nailing shut
Every window and door with pine boards
Which caused Tunstall to angrily shout
And then profane the name of the Lords

Because he didn't have advanced notice
And wanted to remove certain documents
That he needed for trial on the advice
Of McSween who gave skillful arguments

That Tunstalls six horses were omitted
From the attachment and so bought time
To remove them all and being outwitted
A furious Sheriff Brady laid the blame

On McSween who he now wished would rot
In his own jail hardly more than a pit
Lined with rough boards when a thought
Became interrupted and Brady had a fit

Since Deputy Barrier came on the scene
And spoke saying he refused to release
The prisoner to the Sheriff so McSween
Could reside at home with greater ease

So afterwards John Tunstall would open
Up the corral and drive the six horses
To that Feliz Ranch where he would pen
A scathing attack against those forces

By printing in the Independent Gazette
Accusations that charged Sheriff Brady
With taking McSweens taxes which upset
Dolan greatly so that he was all ready

To do anything legal or illegal and so
Published his letter in order to blame
Tunstall for being no gentleman and no
Good but a scoundrel by any other name

The Second Property Attachment

This was one reason why Sheriff Brady
Would send Deputy Matthews instead of
Going himself when they are all ready
To attach Tunstall without much proof

That he and McSween were partners and
The very reason why Matthews traveled
With Jesse Evans leader for that band
Of outlaws in case the plan unraveled

And he would need to call his support
Into action namely Tom Hill and Frank
Baker who are there to back the court
In case Dolans plan starts to go rank

Something which happened on the scene
When Brewer the foreman told him that
These cattle didn't belong to McSween
But to Mr Tunstall a true enough fact

That merely confused the young Deputy
Who was tired and hungry when he said
He'd have to talk about it with Brady
Right now he only wanted to go to bed

Since town was about fifty miles away
And to all of this Dick Brewer agreed
Adding with hospitality they can stay
To share their supper and horses feed

The moment Marshal Widenmann was able
To solve the crime at the Reservation
As soon as they gathered at the table
And then said without much hesitation

The men who stole Indian Agency mules
Were all congregated in the same room
Which in effect had called them fools
And surely made the men who felt doom

Wish they can kill Marshall Widenmann
And probably would've too if Matthews
Had not told them put away their guns
And said the Marshal shouldn't accuse

Innocent men since it made Evans sore
And another cover up his nervous yawn
When with blankets they sleep outdoor
Then in the morning leave before dawn

Matthews Gathers the Posse
26

Right after Billy Matthews had learned
That day he couldn't attach the cattle
When Tunstall protected them he turned
To Dolan who said he would give battle

If they wanted one and so the rustlers
Drifted in from the range to make camp
Near by which slowly but surely alters
The outcome when they enlist any tramp

Who the Seven Rivers Warriors deputize
Along with that Jesse Evans Gang until
The Sheriff's posse swells to the size
Of forty five men whose sole iron will

Was to get Tunstall who was very aware
Of their intentions so sent Bonney and
Waite in town for supplies long before
They came while he rode out and warned

The three Chisum brothers Jeff and Jim
And Pitzer who said their brother John
Wasn't there and then disappointed him
By saying he would have to fight alone

Since John did not want to be involved
In a situation that needed his cowboys
Seeking isolation instead which solved
Nothing while the mutual enemy deploys

At Bob Pauls a ranch twelve miles away
A short distance that could be covered
Across wooded hills in less than a day
Making it difficult when he discovered

Upon arriving back home that the store
Was being too well guarded for his men
Bonney and Waite to stock up with more
Supplies such as rifles and ammunition

Rendering their position mad or insane
But so full of despair he didn't admit
Not even to himself hopes totally wane
And there was nothing to do but submit

But never would because of noble pride
For he was in a long line of ancestors
Whose English blood bolstered his side
Why he couldn't give in to the jesters

Tunstall Decides to Evacuate

But Tunstalls employees prevailed upon
Him to leave the ranch before the dawn
Because an apprehensive John Middleton
Overheard two cowboys telling the yarn

That the posse would come that morning
And so they opened the corral door and
Six horses their hoofs already running
Leaped out and then bolted on the sand

That was the road covered up with snow
Which grew deeper in the mountain pass
Where Bonney and Widenmann together go
Hunting wild turkeys in the tall grass

While Waite coming behind in the wagon
Veered down another road then vanished
Just as Tunstall was telling Middleton
Billy like a horse had to be harnessed

But nevertheless would make a good man
Because he was a source of inspiration
A boy who volunteers to do what he can
So that he becomes a divine revelation

Words that were a remarkable statement
From a man twenty four who would wrest
Out of life a degree of accomplishment
And then heed Greeley's call Come West

Which he would describe in his letters
To his elderly father who would invest
In his dream of succeeding over others
Who failed when character was the test

Of fortunes that rise and fall because
His was rising he said with confidence
To everybody who believed in his cause
And it was in these letters of defense

He boasts to earn half of every dollar
Made in Lincoln County before the year
Was out since he was a finance scholar
Whose excellent thoughts made it clear

How to establish a ring with power and
Awe since everybody needed to have one
Not just for ranching but for any kind
Of occupation or nothing will get done

Murder on the Road to Lincoln

Godfrey Gauss the camp cook was inside
The house when the large posse arrived
To claim the cattle and though he lied
Making Billy Matthews absolutely livid

Since he would not tell where Tunstall
Had gone it made no difference because
They soon saw Tunstalls tracks and all
Of those others who defended his cause

So the posse split up and eighteen men
Under Evans flew down a secondary road
That led to Lincoln through the canyon
Of that wilderness and so quickly rode

They were upon Tunstall before he knew
What to do really except to turn about
And face the posse as a cold wind blew
In his ears and muffled the loud shout

From John Middleton who galloped on by
When Tunstall would say what John what
Even though Middleton had told him why
And he doubtless gave his life so that

Employees had time enough to disappear
So they can run and hide in the forest
When his best horse will suddenly rear
And fall dead with a slug in its chest

Then instantly throw him to the ground
So that he lost breath for how long he
Didn't know but when he did come round
He immediately felt the sting of a bee

Along his arm at the exact same moment
That he had planned to draw his pistol
But was stopped as another bullet sent
Would crack like an egg his bony skull

To make noble blood stain red the snow
Only a few seconds before they carried
And laid his body beside his horse now
To make them look symbolically married

In a sick joke they told about his hat
When setting it on top his horses head
So wayfarers might look and think that
Those sleeping lovers had shared a bed

BOOK TWO

The Coroners Inquest Revealed

After fleeing from the posse Tunstalls
Hired hands rode over to Brewers ranch
And it was here that Middleton recalls
The scene and names those in the bunch

Who had taken part in a crime everyone
There shall abhor and then vow revenge
For a death most cruel before going on
To see McSween in town who will cringe

At the knowledge of his untimely death
And invite them all to spend the night
While he pants as though out of breath
In preparation with the upcoming fight

That loomed up in the distance between
Himself and James Dolan and John Riley
Who had come to hate Alexander McSween
Soon after he had moved to that valley

And so McSween made sure the mortician
John Newcomb left his house in Lincoln
With four Mexicans to climb a mountain
For hours until they uncover a body on

The highway where Middleton remembered
And found their exact location somehow
Tunstall and his horse which slumbered
With all four limbs buried in the snow

When they set him up on the mules back
Then tied ropes to prevent his falling
And then retraced the exact same track
To where a Coroner Inquest was meeting

At the Ellis House with duly appointed
Justice of the Peace John Wilson a man
Who was honest and really disappointed
When witnesses questioned on the stand

Sadly revealed each murderers identity
To the court so that he made Constable
Martinez put aside their bitter enmity
To select volunteers who are most able

To keep the laws and made him deputize
Bonney and Waite to help join the fray
Hoping to cut the Sheriff down in size
Because he was stealing Tunstall's hay

Sheriff Brady Resists Arrest

So Constable Atanacio Martinez planned
To arrest Sheriff William Brady before
He could resist everyone and be warned
By people who shopped inside the store

A plan so strange and full of audacity
It would fail miserably long before he
Entered a room under the full capacity
Of western law to arrest Sheriff Brady

Aided by Fred Waite and William Bonney
Who tried to sneak in the room unheard
And then in a situation that was funny
Were arrested by Sheriff Brady instead

With the help of none other than Baker
And Morton who were wanted at the time
By Martinez for John Tunstall's murder
But were never charged with that crime

On account of Sheriff Brady who stated
They had shot Tunstall in self defense
An unlikely story since they had hated
Tunstall and none of it made any sense

Specially when the testimony of others
Who were all eyewitnesses at the scene
Said they could identify those killers
Morton and Baker who became awful mean

As they suddenly removed their weapons
And marched them before the whole town
To the jail a dug pit where it happens
A crowd came with a disapproving frown

Once Bonney shouted you son of a bitch
After Morton and Baker with wood slats
Tried to turn aside water from a ditch
Into the hole and drown them like rats

And surely would have if not for Brady
Who yelled and told them to leave town
Because he was afraid that a war party
Made of sympathizers might come around

The reason he let Martinez out of jail
But kept two Deputies Bonney and Waite
Detained without a chance to post bail
Forcing them to endure an unknown fate

Sebrian Bates Hears a Ghost

Sebrian Bates the black house servant
Stomped both of his boots in the cold
And then stopped for a minute to pant
Before resuming the thing he was told

By McSween which was to dig the grave
In the ground behind Tunstall's store
Where everything was pitch black save
For a lantern light that made a score

Of dark shadows dance across the snow
Whenever wind blew and shook the tree
Until Sebrian trembled in fear anyhow
As on the day each slave was set free

When his world was turned upside down
Then as now with Tunstall in a coffin
Suited and embalmed and yet not shown
Due to a rifle butt breaking his chin

And wound in his skull two of a dozen
Examined by Dr Appel the army surgeon
Who found the corpse was still frozen
When he arrived there from Ft Stanton

For the post mortem and warmly washed
The body clean with soap by the fires
When he probed for lead balls smashed
Against bone with his surgical pliers

The tragedy Sebrian knew could happen
To McSween too who stuck out his neck
Once again when he walked in the open
Alongside Martinez this time to check

Sheriff Brady in checkers for the hay
He had stolen out of Tunstall's store
As he tried again and succeeded today
In arresting him for taking even more

When just then he heard a screech owl
And becoming afraid he hurried inside
Because he believed this was the howl
Of a ghost and in his room would hide

Pulling the blankets up over his head
When once again he had heard Tunstall
Say whooooo killed me since I am dead
Scary sounds that made his skin crawl

The Funeral of John Tunstall
32

Friday three o'clock the funeral began
When a huge crowd stood up in the room
And sang religious hymns Susan McSween
Played on her piano to a sense of doom

Since everyone already knew the reason
Tunstall's coffin lid remained covered
So people could not see his expression
Was because he got maimed and murdered

Another reason why so many women there
Had white handkerchiefs in their hands
To daub tearful eyes while taking care
To fix mussed hair a few loose strands

As they listened to the new missionary
Mr Ealy quote from the big black bible
A man McSween had deemed was necessary
During these times of terrible trouble

Believing a Reverend should be invited
Because Lincoln had not built a church
When suddenly some people grew excited
At seeing those four pallbearers lurch

Down the aisle carrying a heavy coffin
With a large flag covering up the body
Until they went outdoor and laid it in
The ground where Sebrian and everybody

Formed rows about five feet deep there
Within a space next to the stores wall
When they heard Brewer violently swear
He would revenge the death of Tunstall

A neighbor and friend even if it meant
He had to track down all the murderers
To kill them startling news that leant
Melancholy airs and caused townfathers

To reexamine Sheriff Brady's testimony
Immediately after the funeral was over
When he was asked why Waite and Bonney
Were in jail and said he had the power

To hold anyone he pleased then got rid
Of everyone in the room with an excuse
Saying he had to go at once and so hid
From the townfathers with a false ruse

They Become the Regulators

When Tunstalls employees realized that
Sheriff Brady would not make an arrest
For the murder and as a matter of fact
He insisted the posse was like a beast

With claws that reacts in self defense
When its confronted with sudden danger
Dick Brewer would not sit on the fence
Uncertain what to do but said in anger

Justice Wilson appointed him constable
The reason he would ask each volunteer
In the crowd at McSweens kitchen table
To help track those killers everywhere

And so backed by some rich benefactors
He created a posse of some fifteen men
Giving them the name of the Regulators
When something happened so very sudden

Rob Widenmann returned from Ft Stanton
And brought twenty five black soldiers
All led by Lieutenant Goodwin only one
Of the seven privileged white officers

Inside this fort who did not interfere
With Brewers Regulators who now arrest
Five Deputies guarding Tunstalls store
All men who the Regulators will attest

Have stolen hay from the loft and once
Removed from power leave the door open
For Bonney and Waite to happily bounce
From the jail where they were so often

Mistreated by the guards but were free
Now to join up with the Regulators who
Were assisted by troops in some degree
But had mostly been independent though

Since the troops had come to apprehend
The Evans Gang for stealing government
Mules off Mescalero Indian Agency land
But a search found none and this meant

The soldiers had to return to the fort
After having been in town only one day
A disappointment to black soldiers for
Everyone liked town and wanted to stay

The Regulators are Arrested
34

On the day preceding Sheriff Brady was
Arrested for stealing hay and released
On bond and then five Deputies because
Of the same thing so it only increased

His hatred toward Brewer who organized
The resistance against him when he put
His five men in jail until he realized
What happened and then bailed them out

And so a little later on when he heard
Brewer's posse was meeting at McSweens
U shaped house in order to spread word
Of an insurrection this at first seems

Difficult for Sheriff Brady to believe
Until he brought Deputies he had there
To arrest them for rioting and relieve
Them of weapons and in what was a rare

Mood of laughter recognize the obvious
There were too many prisoners for jail
And so Brady was given the non envious
Task of letting everyone leave on bail

Then wait for the spring term of court
But since James Dolan became impatient
He raced to La Mesilla hoping to abort
The future and surprise to some extent

Everyone when he raced back to Lincoln
With an alias warrant that would allow
McSween to become incarcerated by noon
A bold plan indeed and one sure to sow

Even larger strife among the residents
Who were actually pleased to see Dolan
Return to find the U shaped apartments
Locked and McSween nowhere to be found

Having been last seen leaving the town
Early that morning with Deputy Barrier
Who was sending him to a place unknown
Because McSween's position was so dire

Now that the politically powerful ring
In Santa Fe wished him dead and buried
And demonstrated a will to do anything
Irregardless if justice was miscarried

The Regulators in Hot Pursuit

About March six eighteen seventy eight
Brewers posse rode in the back country
Where they hope to find and then fight
The Jesse Evans Gang who they will try

To apprehend after Bonneys helpful tip
That leads to the gangs secret hideout
At Rio Penasco where their horses slip
Up the steep bank after Bonney's shout

And extended arm revealed the position
Of five men sitting under a large tree
Who jumped for the horses on detection
Then flew down the road hoping to flee

The posse which closed in on the chase
Then pressed them so hard with gunfire
They split into as they can't out race
Brewers posse who with a single desire

Made a beeline for three men who start
To turn left and so let two men escape
Who keep to the right but fire so that
Cowboy Dick Lloyd gets a bloody scrape

On his nose as his wounded horse falls
Head over hoofs but nothing much worse
Because the serious posse never stalls
Or pauses at any time from this course

Of pursuit since these men were Morgan
And Baker whose wounded horses stumble
After awhile and force them to bargain
With Dick Brewer who will soon grumble

When he threatens to burn scrub bushes
Where they hide and will say very grim
He wants them dead and actually wishes
They didn't surrender so easily to him

Since he too feels rage over Tunstalls
Death at their hands and then displays
Much courage or another way male balls
By deflecting Bonney's aim as he plays

Russian roulette and points the barrel
Up at Morgans temple and then squeezes
The trigger before mounting his sorrel
And all of that tension suddenly eases

The Regulators Take Prisoners

Later on in the evening they made camp
When Brewer gave the prisoners a guard
Doing this so the men could not escape
But also since there was little regard

For these mens well being in the posse
Which set out the next morning at dawn
With the attitude of lets wait and see
What happens when they will reach town

Which was still at least two days ride
From there and so halted for breakfast
At Gilberts Ranch and then once inside
Meet William McCloskey who in the past

Worked for Tunstall and this McCloskey
Who headed in the same direction there
Asked Brewer if he can join that posse
Along its journey and so Brewer a fair

Man in all things said to him I reckon
Theres no harm since Brewer understood
McCloskey had some business in Lincoln
And so left with the posse which would

Finally at sun down reach South Spring
Yet another ranch owned by John Chisum
Who during consultation let them bring
In both prisoners who looked very glum

According to Sally Chisum John's niece
Who had to relinquish her bedroom that
Night for security and did things nice
When she brought them meat without fat

And plenty of potatoes on their plates
Before she ever thought to get herself
Supper because she had generous traits
Like her Uncle John who prided himself

On being able to set a bountiful table
That would be enough to satisfy twenty
Hungry men at one sitting and was able
To provide beds for at least that many

Sleepy cowboys who took turns guarding
The prisoners every two hours at night
Knowing beforehand they were departing
When dawn shimmered in the first light

The Regulators Take Rest

After the meal Chisum took the leaders
Of the posse to his office for a drink
Pouring the liquor into glass tumblers
With a lit cigar that helped him think

Back to when he first settled the area
With his three brothers back to a time
When the Indians had ruined his career
When stealing a mans horse was a crime

Punishable by death since he would die
Without a horse in this big sky desert
Where a man on foot was fit to be tied
Or one man all alone had to stay alert

Like McSween now that Tunstall was out
Of the picture that John Chisum was in
Probably up to his neck or there about
And liked to be without and not within

Which is why he asked Hunter and Evans
Cattle Company to send their detective
Frank MacNab to catch that Jesse Evans
And his gang who were really effective

At rustling his steers from the plains
That were bought off Charlie Goodnight
Now with more than enough blood stains
Trying to hold what was his in a fight

That had come right onto his door step
Into his livingroom and now his office
Where these men looked to him for help
And the least he could do was act nice

When he told them a rumor he had heard
And said James Dolan got it from Upton
What you boys were up to and is headed
This way with his posse to meet you on

The main road from Lincoln and advised
Them to use a less traveled road there
Like Agua Negra Canyon and so realized
How Chisum now stood and would compare

Notes with one another without telling
McCloskey about it so that he remained
In the dark over how they were feeling
Since his relationship became strained

The Regulators Take Revenge
38

At night both men will compose letters
Morgan to his family on the East Coast
An educated man who wrote with fetters
To say what happened leaving the worst

Parts off and Baker to his girl friend
Who he gives his wallet and gold watch
Even though this delivery shall depend
On Sally Chisum who they quickly catch

That morning around the breakfast bell
Before they leave there with the posse
And then start for the town of Roswell
With the blond girls fragrance of rose

Perfume faint in their noses so Morgan
Can mail his letter at the post office
Where Ash Upton the stores clerk began
To feel concerned for Morgan and twice

Asked whether the boys would be killed
Before they reach Lincoln as McCloskey
Who stood beside Morgan became chilled
And said if they do over his dead body

This exclamation heard by Frank MacNab
The cattle agent Hunter and Evans sent
To Chisum hoping rustlers he might nab
Just before they mounted and then went

North along the road bound for Lincoln
Or at least McCloskey thought so until
The posse turned for Agua Negra Canyon
Where McCloskey became perfectly still

While MacNab shouted so you're the son
Of a bitch who's got to die and pulled
The trigger so that he lost his reason
On the instant his brains were spilled

Like crimson cauliflower on the ground
Because taken from behind in the skull
Causing prisoners to bolt at the sound
So Bonney and the posse instantly pull

Weapons and shoot them from the saddle
Before they can escape down the canyon
Where they would roll and rocks rattle
Then halt not far from their companion

The Regulators Become Outlaws

Afterwards each man in the posse swore
To keep what happened here a secret on
Pain of death a deed of blood and gore
Before they rode from the small canyon

Leaving the three bodies on the ground
For the bears and coyotes and buzzards
Before hitting a long trail that wound
Up the steep wall with certain hazards

Which took them to the Mexican village
Of San Patricio and where with friends
They waited until Brewer pacing a cage
For a few days grows restless and ends

His stay there when he goes to Lincoln
With Bonney who becomes like a partner
And hears a posse has found the canyon
With the three bodies from the coroner

Who came to examine them and found six
Bullet holes in Baker but eleven holes
In Morgan also saying a posse will fix
The murderers when Sheriff Brady rolls

Out of town on their trail a statement
Made to him so casually he would learn
Its significance and see what it meant
Only after someone they know will warn

Them about the fact that Sheriff Brady
Would arrest them when they go outside
And so used a back door of the Waverly
Hotel not knowing some posse will hide

Near there and they will have to shoot
Their way out running up to the corral
To jump on the horses when Billys boot
Heel takes a bullet and will soon fall

In the road on which they shall escape
From that posse who calls them outlaws
Since Gov Axtell hearing of the scrape
That had happened told President Hayes

Who then gave him permission to remove
Brewers constabulary authority granted
Him by Justice Wilson a dastardly move
That made all of the Regulators hunted

Jesse Evans Finally Arrested
40

It was at around this time Jesse Evans
Along with partner Tom Hill would stop
At John Wagner's camp where some plans
Turned out better than they could hope

Being able to come in with nobody home
A situation preferred by these thieves
Who are in no hurry and so slowly comb
Through the big room until Evans spies

A rifle that hangs above the fireplace
That he steals finding it irresistible
And so then starts to leave that place
When through a window he spots trouble

In the form of some blanketed Cherokee
A shepherd who left his flock of sheep
Lying in the meadow under a shade tree
To protect the cabin and climbed steep

Embankments before being shot by Evans
Who knocked him down in the tall grass
While a bullet that hit his leg stains
His moccasins with blood but will pass

Through exactly when Evans was telling
Hill they would celebrate with a toast
Later on when Tom left without knowing
That the Indian stood next to the post

When once outside he was shot to death
By his own rifle that the Cherokee had
Removed from his scabbard with stealth
Without scaring the horses in the yard

Where Evans put one leg out the window
And then the other and so had to fight
The Cherokee every step of the way now
For him to escape when he would alight

On his horse with a left elbow smashed
Into by a bullet so that he would need
Treatment at Ft Stanton when he dashed
Down the road going at breakneck speed

And then ran right into Constable Wood
Who arrested then took him to hospital
Where the army doctors fixed his wound
Then guards came to lock Evans in jail

McSween Shows Up at Chisums

After awhile townspeople wondered what
Happened to McSween on the day that he
And Deputy Barrier vanished after that
Time they quarreled with Sheriff Brady

Because some said they were hiding out
Somewhere in the Capitan Mountains for
The next term in the spring when court
Opens up its doors but this was before

Someone heard McSween and Barrier were
Staying at Chisum's South Spring Ranch
And that McSween was soon joined there
By his wife Susan who arrived at lunch

After coming all the way from St Louis
On the stage because some said she had
Taken monies from the bank and so this
Was the reason why their curtain shade

Was now drawn tight over their windows
Because they were afraid and everybody
Knew this and knew Sheriff Brady shows
Up there to arrest McSween with a body

Of troops under leadership of Lt Smith
Who instantly sees how violent clashes
Between Brady and McSween aren't myths
But realities that he patiently hashes

Out by sending Susan into her husbands
Room after he flatly refused to appear
With a brief message that soon demands
His surrender then guarantees in clear

Unambiguous language a military escort
To Ft Stanton where he shall be placed
Under house arrest until the new court
When McSween feigning sickness refused

To see them or come out of his bedroom
And instead worked out this compromise
That he would come to the fort as soon
As he can ride and so McSweens promise

Was duly accepted by Lt Smith who took
All of his soldiers back to Ft Stanton
Even though Brady will resist and look
Immovable like statues of marble stone

An Ambush for Sheriff Brady
42

So McSween was ordered to come himself
Before the court was scheduled to open
But with the mischievousness of an elf
Spring rain made sure it didn't happen

When roads mired in unfortunate floods
Caused McSween's party to take shelter
At a Hondo ranch which upset the moods
Of everyone who left there a day later

Too late to meet the prior arrangement
With Lt Smith who returned to the fort
But would reappear for the arraignment
Irregardless on the first day of court

That resumed during the month of April
When seven armed Regulators would meet
Behind Tunstalls store waiting to kill
Sheriff Brady who came down the street

One hour before noon to arrest McSween
As soon as he showed at the courthouse
Not knowing men would shoot in between
Two buildings during a surprise ambush

At the second he stepped in their view
Or he would fall dead with nine bullet
Holes while Deputy Hindmann with a few
In his chest was alive still and upset

When he glimpsed Bonney and Jim French
And saw Bonney lean over Sheriff Brady
To search his vest and suddenly wrench
An alias warrant in his pocket already

Having picked up his confiscated rifle
That had fallen from Brady to the dirt
One like new and marked up very little
After he wiped the mud on Bradys shirt

Not realizing until he heard two shots
From Deputy Matthews who was hiding in
The Cisneros house there might be lots
More Deputies about and so that's when

He heard a scream from Big Jim who was
Shot in the rear then had to be helped
With one arm over his shoulder because
He didn't limp to the store but hopped

Deputy Hindmanns Nightmare

Meanwhile in the silence that followed
Right after the battle the new teacher
Closed the one room school and allowed
All of the children to file passed her

Out the door with a strict instruction
Not to go near the street or the scene
But certain boys for further education
Disobeyed and then rushed over to lean

Against a white fence with abject fear
At seeing the two bodies of the lawmen
Lying so helplessly on the street near
Puddles of rain water then of a sudden

Watched as a man runs over to the side
Of Deputy Hindmann who cried for water
And soon after drinking it did confide
To him that he saw the Devil and later

Slipped into a dream or sort of memory
Remembering the time he shot at a bear
A giant grizzly according to the story
Of Sebrian black servant who was there

And would tell anyone who would listen
How the bear would charge for Hindmann
Knock him sideways with a paw and then
Gnaw at his hand and give a belly moan

Because six gunshots crippled its guts
Yet never slowed down the grizzlys run
And he lost blood through so many cuts
Sebrian had no choice but fire his gun

Making that bear chase and then follow
Him up a tall tree he started to climb
When his boots stuck in the mud hollow
With the grizzly bear right behind him

So that from terror Sebrian would yell
I's a gonna Lord dat bear gonna eat me
But didn't want to live a life in hell
So the bear climbed back down the tree

And then once again gnawed at the hand
Of Hindmann until it departed his side
Leaving him with only one good arm and
No luck left this time because he died

Bonney Rescues Big Jim French

The wound in his buttocks hurt so much
Big Jim French found he could not ride
And using his rifle stock for a crutch
Bonney helped him find a place to hide

Under the floor of Tunstalls apartment
Where the clerk Sam Corbet still lived
And covered a trap door with parchment
While Bonney ran back and then strived

To engage two of those Deputies Peppin
And Matthews and then shot Deputy Long
Hitting his upper leg before he ran in
The Torreon a stone tower built strong

Enough by the Spanish to stand against
Indian raids during earlier days until
His companions signaled on the instant
He looked up at them it was their will

To leave that place and held the reins
Meanwhile as Bonney booted the stirrup
Swung in the saddle and suddenly gains
The lead in front of riders who gallop

Away like the wind before the Deputies
Came from hiding to search Sam Corbets
Apartment since they knew the injuries
Were serious and so even Matthews bets

They'll soon see Jim but was surprised
When they came up empty handed and had
To stop checking since nobody realized
He was below the floor bleeding so bad

He felt a little faint but much better
At following their departure since Sam
Had found a rag for a tourniquet after
When he bolted the lock but took alarm

Much later on that night when a sudden
Knock heard upon the door would reveal
That smile of William Bonney just then
Whose style it was to borrow not steal

Two poles and a blanket from an Indian
Pulling the stretcher behind his horse
Which helped him to carry away Big Jim
Afterwards in total darkness of course

Alex McSween Turns Himself In

When the McSween party arrived in town
Soon after the murders had taken place
Deputy Peppin determinedly rushed down
With Deputy Matthews to summarily face

And then arrest McSween with the alias
Warrant but to their amazement McSween
Had already surrendered to Lt Smith as
That army officer controlled the scene

With some twenty five buffalo soldiers
Placed all around his house plus eight
More who stood on the roof with orders
From Lt Smith to freely shoot on sight

Anyone they saw who might harm McSween
Who felt as surprised at what happened
As anyone there and was caught between
Two warring factions when court opened

The first day of April but then closed
Because Judge Bristol had cancelled it
After he believed that a session posed
New danger for himself if he would sit

And then preside on the bench as usual
And so there was nothing they could do
Except follow an army procedure manual
That took McSween and David Shield too

With them when they would return again
To beloved Fort Stanton where the pair
Felt unbelievable humiliation and pain
Because they would be held in the care

Of jailors until private quarters were
Offered within rooms of barest comfort
Until April eighth and must stay there
Within the strict confines of the fort

Since Attorney Rynerson the prosecutor
Had refused to accept payment of bonds
And became instead a hellish tormentor
Though the gentlemen own wealthy lands

And could easily afford to buy freedom
If the choice had been offered to them
So McSween wished the heavenly kingdom
Would descend with Christ in Jerusalem

The Battle with Buckshot Rogers
46

When the Regulators led by Dick Brewer
Reached Blazers Mill a road side house
At around noon they went in for dinner
After posting two guards there because

Joseph Blazer rubbing his bearded face
Told them the troops from Fort Stanton
Had recently come through to his place
As had Buckshot Rogers who followed on

Their trail and so this was the reason
Why John Middleton and George Coe were
Seated on the porch already for action
Having drawn and cocked a rifle hammer

When suddenly they glimpse past a rail
Buckshot Rogers coming in a huge cloud
Of dust that rose high above the trail
And could tell right away he was proud

Hoping to fight as he slowed to a stop
Around thirty feet away from the porch
Where he would leave his mule and prop
A rifle butt on a boot and then slouch

When Frank Coe a sometime friend moved
Around the corner and sat in a doorway
With Buckshot to negotiate what proved
Useless since he wanted things his way

So that's when Brewer asked volunteers
Bonney and Bowdre one other George Coe
To arrest him and rope him like steers
And around a corner they would soon go

With Bowdre taking the lead cautiously
When Rogers rifle fired on the instant
Causing Bowdre to shoot simultaneously
And pierce Rogers gut so he would pant

Yelling now at Bowdre no way Mary Anne
Although the bullet ricocheted at once
Off Bowdres buckle right onto the hand
Of George Coe his trigger finger slice

Off just seconds before Middleton shot
Wildly then missed his mark as Roberts
Hit his chest making the name Buckshot
Mean a diehard fighter who never quits

Dick Brewer Dies in the Battle

With so many men wounded in that fight
Dick Brewer no longer wanted to arrest
Buckshot Rogers but shoot him on sight
The moment he saw the man who now rest

On a bed mattress he laid on the floor
Since in addition Roberts had ambushed
Bonney and Bowdre only the week before
And was the reason they quickly rushed

At Roberts even though Bonney remained
Behind the wall not venturing out till
Brewer gestured his hand and explained
He planned to move down by the sawmill

And so they crossed over a foot bridge
Whose stream drove a wood paddle wheel
And reached a pile of logs at the edge
Of Blazers mill where Dick in his zeal

Watched for movement within the window
Raised his rifle to shoot it and later
Peered with his head over the logs now
As Roberts would take aim and splatter

Brewers brain with an old sharps rifle
He removed from a wall and then loaded
Roberts aware that nothing will stifle
His wild laughter which plainly goaded

As Brewer fell backward instantly dead
A surprise that made Bonney reconsider
His action even more since others said
Blazer affirmed Roberts must go yonder

In one day with his wounds an argument
Which seemed reasonable and encouraged
Them to listen without further comment
When Blazer said he had urgently paged

Doctor Daniel Appel over at Ft Stanton
Who planned to meet with them half way
Along the road where that army surgeon
Dressed wounds received during the day

Which brought the Regulators criticism
Afterwards for having left Dick Brewer
With Blazer who showed little cynicism
By burying both men beside one another

The Trial of Alexander McSween
48

When court began early in the morning
Of April eighth the crowd at the door
Couldn't find enough room for sitting
In the chairs and so filled the floor

Standing all the way to the back wall
Where some dog laid by the wood stove
Dreaming its dreams not caring at all
About the jury selections which drove

Judge Bristol crazy since he couldn't
Find enough people who felt impartial
Since most folks in the town wouldn't
Badly affect the outcome of the trial

But help swing it in favor of McSween
Good folks too like Doc Joseph Blazer
Jury leader and Juan Patron both seen
To be men with minds sharp as a razor

Who disliked Bristol telling the jury
In hearing of David Shield his lawyer
McSween could be charged with perjury
When he proved his client was no liar

With the witnesses who took the stand
Representing the Spiegelberg Brothers
Who said they could easily understand
Why he had acted this way when others

Had misrepresented even misunderstood
McSweens purpose for showing in court
And in their opinion he had done good
By bringing everyone there to account

And to further bolster their argument
They presented the original bank loan
Into evidence a small yellow document
That quickly made the prosecutor moan

District Attorney Rynerson as soon as
The jury wandered in from adjournment
To tell everyone that the verdict was
Not guilty on charges of embezzlement

An announcement that hushed the crowd
Who struggled with what had been said
Then chimed in as one by saying aloud
What good is it for Tunstall was dead

The Decisions of Lincoln County
49

When McSween was acquitted by the jury
The men responsible for John Tunstalls
Murder were so afraid of bodily injury
They sought protection for one and all

At Ft Stanton from where they ventured
Frequently to attend those proceedings
Of weekly court Judge Bristol censured
Since Dolans defense wasn't succeeding

And indeed failed or literally stalled
When Jesse Evans and three accomplices
Were charged in the murder of Tunstall
With Dolan and Matthews as accessories

Making each pay a five thousand dollar
Bond that Dolan and Matthews could pay
But which Evans like a dog on a collar
Let others pay before Murphy went away

To seek his protection at Fort Stanton
Where because he has many army friends
He will convince Col Dudley to abandon
McSweens position because he has means

To bring about that groups destruction
Namely Billy Bonney who the grand jury
Charged along with Brown and Middleton
For the wanton murder of Sheriff Brady

And Waite for shooting Deputy Hindmann
All others unmentioned for some reason
When that jury named Bowdre as the man
Who murdered Rogers in another session

And named Regulators at Blazer's mills
Accessories to the murder then finally
Indicted in what became a war of wills
Leaders from the house Dolan and Riley

On charges of stealing Chisum's cattle
Which they sold the Indian Reservation
But witnesses were unwilling to tattle
And added to peoples great frustration

Until no one had a choice and everyone
Needed to pick one side over the other
As the town became divided and the gun
Replaced the law as the dominant power

Frank MacNab Dies in Ambush
50

When it became known that Frank MacNab
Cattle detective from Hunter and Evans
Had taken Brewer's place and would nab
More of the rustlers like Jessie Evans

The gang of Seven Rivers Warriors rode
To the Fritz's Ranch to wait in ambush
Until MacNab was spotted down the road
With two other men who they would rush

Frank Coe and young cousin Ab Saunders
Who took bullets in the ankle and side
Above his hip so quick that Ab wonders
What happened as Frank ran off to hide

In an arroyo and fight it out with Bob
Olinger until his bullets were no more
And he surrendered giving Frank MacNab
The time he needed by opening the door

For his escape around the small spring
Where they had stopped to water horses
And he hung his arm with a cloth sling
Badly wounded by Marion Turners forces

Who amounted to twenty five men in all
That also would include Indian Segovia
Who guarded MacNab when he would crawl
Away while down on hands and knees via

A path that went into a clump of trees
That the half breed could easily trace
Where MacNab swung around on his knees
At the moment a gun blast hit his face

Killing him instantly although unarmed
Before moving back to rejoin the group
That for some reason left Coe unharmed
As four Warriors will strain and stoop

To pick up Ab Saunders who cannot walk
And then carry him to the Fritzs house
Where they argue together as they talk
About Ft Stanton since he needs a dose

Of medicine and someone to mend wounds
From which Saunders unfortunately dies
About nine months later without sounds
In the room among the buzzing of flies

The All Day Long Battle in Town

When the Seven Rivers Warriors arrived
In Lincoln with the prisoner Frank Coe
Who felt really lucky to have survived
After he was searched from head to toe

They all gathered over at Dolans store
To inform John Copland the new sheriff
What had happened when a sudden uproar
Came from outside and they wondered if

This was a good morning surprise party
Designed by Regulators and sure enough
Everybody bolted from the room already
Leaving Frank Coe who started to cough

Uncontrollably because Willard Olinger
Bobs brother said he didn't like being
Left out and so would join his brother
And with the kindness of a human being

Surprised Frank Coe by handing his gun
Back to him in case he met someone who
Was less generous and so Coe would run
Out the back door so nobody would know

And then amble over to the Ellis House
Where he came without further incident
And realized this situation more worse
Than before and so grew less confident

In the Regulator's ability to hold off
A larger force that held half the town
So that all of his friends would scoff
At his temerity and say they would own

Lincoln by this time tomorrow but when
In fact it was ridiculous and everyone
Realized it was impossible to win even
Though brother George Coe had that gun

That marksmanship of which he was king
And showed it from the top of the roof
By smashing both legs of Dutch Kruling
A distance four hundred yards as proof

Because it was really the soldiers who
Ended the fight after Sheriff Copeland
Wired Lt Smith saying he needed a coup
To restore peace to this frontier land

MacNabs Murderers Wander Away

Sheriff Copeland arrested the Warriors
As many as he could find but could not
Take the guns without creating uproars
From Marion Turner who would've fought

To keep them and so they struck a deal
The Warriors can keep their weapons if
They will return with troops an appeal
That eases all burden from the Sheriff

Until McSween arrives from the Mexican
Town of San Patricio claiming warrants
For the murderers of MacNab which came
From Justice Trujillo who really wants

Copland to hurry up over to Ft Stanton
Where they roam freely and arrest them
A task much more easily said than done
Since Col Dudley believes this problem

Needs to be reversed and asks Copeland
And Lt Smith to take along some troops
To hunt down McSween for what happened
Earlier in town since Col Dudley hopes

Murphy was right when he had intimated
McSween was nothing except bad trouble
Making all the townspeople intimidated
So they overtook McSween on the double

And then marched him with seven others
Back to Ft Stanton where he was thrown
In a small cell so crowded it smothers
Everyone even his black servant a pawn

In the game that will upset Col Dudley
When he hears the law required McSween
Be shipped to San Patricio immediately
Because good Justice Trujillo had been

Adamant for their correct jurisdiction
A move that presented Sheriff Copeland
With a big problem since proper action
Required their return and he apprehend

The Warriors but about this Col Dudley
Refused and so there was nothing to do
But release all the parties as quickly
As possible during a sudden hullabaloo

Murphy Leaves Dolan Everything

For a long time afterwards townspeople
Gave various answers as to the reasons
Why Lawrence Murphys health was feeble
And made his will since he had no sons

Naming James Dolan as sole beneficiary
But after awhile there was a consensus
That said Murphy could no longer carry
The burdens of being a probate Justice

Because he got the disease consumption
Which some ladies in the town ascribed
To several wicked vices the assumption
Being cigars and liquor put him to bed

Early each night but these accusations
Were all unfounded according to Murphy
Even though Dr Appel at Fort Stanton's
Hospital had said the muscular atrophy

He feared came from an internal cancer
And would recommend that Murphy travel
To Santa Fe since he might find answer
For a health problem and there unravel

The mystery because medicine practiced
On the frontier was crude at very best
And so then on May tenth as he noticed
Dolan and Longwell had sufficient rest

They started out together for Santa Fe
Feeling very nervous being on the road
Because McSween would pay anyone a fee
Of five thousand for any wretched toad

Who helped murder John Tunstall Junior
Money he acquired from written letters
All to his father John Tunstall Senior
And so this was why Murphy had jitters

And he looked over his shoulder before
Leaving the fort after he caught sight
Of Doc Scurlock coming out of the door
Thinking they might anticipate a fight

Since Billy the Kid was doubtless near
His gang could jump them along the way
A situation that filled them with fear
Until they safely reached old Santa Fe

The Regulators Kill Indian Segovia
54

When Doc Scurlock got back to Lincoln
And learned the Warriors stole horses
Off the Tunstall ranch they travel on
To Seven Rivers to recover the losses

By raiding the Dolan and Riley cattle
Camp that was there without realizing
They sold everything the whole kettle
Of beans as it were to that analyzing

Silver tongued businessman Tom Catron
Who held Dolans mortgage in the store
Also all the purse strings of Lincoln
And soon as he heard became damn sore

About the fact they took twenty seven
Horses from his cattle camp and would
Definitely find some ways to get even
Say killing them if he possibly could

After he learnt they found the Indian
Segovia hiding out alone at his place
And then executed him in that Mexican
Style putting a bandana over his face

Then a bullet in the back of his head
While he sat on his knees in the dirt
Begged for life but got death instead
After being seen asleep with no shirt

Where he took siesta in the small bed
As customary to ease a scorching heat
On that afternoon or he would've fled
To perhaps lived long enough to cheat

Some other Mexican out of a few pesos
And then kill him because he was mean
As when he shot MacNab with no pathos
So his vaulted exploits could be seen

By the gringo as a sign of friendship
Worthy of praise and ten silver coins
While in reality this they would skip
And give him whiskey and a few onions

Which he would eat and drink and pass
Out from after lying on the small bed
His dreams disturbed by obnoxious gas
Never realizing he would soon be dead

McSween Recruits a Large Posse

Feeling much despair and out of touch
With God when he arrived in the small
Hamlet of San Patricio the one church
Seemed like a true magnet to the tall

Lawyer who now entered the dark booth
To offer his confession to the priest
For forgiveness that seemed to soothe
His worried mind so he could at least

Walk back through the huge twin doors
Squinting up his eyes in the sunlight
At the horse which stood on all fours
Still waiting there for him to alight

And then once he was up in the saddle
Ride from there with Sheriff Copeland
To the next town where a sweet fiddle
Was featured over guitars in the band

Of musicians who enlivened the saloon
With their folk music in a room where
Girls on the sidelines dance and soon
Bonney and a group of Mexicans appear

To start shooting a game of billiards
And then afterwards offer free drinks
To anyone who had a new deck of cards
When McSween shouted if anyone thinks

We're here to have fun they are wrong
And put an end to happiness instantly
As he stood in front and then went on
Talking and then said rather candidly

Whoever fights Murphy Dolan and Riley
And by doing helps take back the town
Will have food and compensation daily
And rewards not with money of his own

But from Tunstall's prosperous estate
Something which the Mexicans urgently
Needed till they heard Copeland state
The dreaded news that he had recently

Been forced out of his lofty position
As Sheriff by Mr Peppin after a saucy
Judge Bristol appointed a new mission
Designed to kill the Regulators posse

The Two Battles of San Patricio

When the Regulators rode into the town
Of San Patricio later on that same day
A posse that they could not have known
Had warrants quickly and without delay

Began to shoot at them from a distance
Which the Regulators would narrow down
By creating an impossible circumstance
That forced the Deputies to leave town

Since Long's horse was shot and killed
After a running battle late in the day
Which gave them confidence and stilled
The town but not Longs voice when they

Followed a road that led to Ft Stanton
And spoke to Dudley who heard the case
With growing alarm and then decided on
Action and so acted like a horse's ass

On account he wasn't supposed to order
Twenty five boys under Captain Carroll
To join the posse at the towns boarder
And realizing his mistake would recall

The troops since a Posse Comitatus Act
Stated without doubt that the army had
Few granted powers to adversely impact
Civilians and made any future look bad

For Deputy Baca and for Sheriff Peppin
Who rode to San Patricio on July third
And were met by an unwelcome reception
From the Regulators who claimed a bird

Told them a large posse was on its way
Then released such a storm of elements
From rooftops the posse would not stay
But quickly retreated in a few moments

After they lost two horses in the hail
And Julian Lopez got his arm shattered
Because someone's shotgun fired a nail
As they left town not that it mattered

To the dozen or so poor naked children
Who with barking dogs came from houses
To stand on an empty street and listen
The only sound cries of wounded horses

A Posse Pursues the Regulators

Because Chisum wants them to celebrate
The fourth of July inside his ranchero
The Regulators flirt unaware with fate
When they would head for the Rio Hondo

Then spot a posse four miles from town
Because of a dust cloud on the horizon
That indicated Kinneys posse had grown
From insignificance to about two dozen

And shall include Dolan and Peppin too
The very reason why McSween shall wait
For the posse to slowly come into view
Before using high ridges to annihilate

Two of their horses and then send them
Running back to San Patricio in a rout
Where Kinney blamed this whole problem
On McSween and wished to drive him out

By first shooting the windows in homes
And then by tearing off the store roof
With lassos so next time McSween comes
Citizens might act a little more aloof

Knowing if they do help him their town
Shall soon become mere rubble and dust
And to further have their message sown
Seeing no souls in whom they can trust

The posse stole tequila from the store
And drank it until they all were drunk
Enough to treat one woman like a whore
Proving once again these dogs had sunk

Even lower than the beasts taking what
They want having no concern for others
Shooting holes in one mans Mexican hat
After Christ said all men are brothers

And generally terrorizing this village
Before they left late in the afternoon
Nearly killing a senile man of old age
Because a wild horse ran over him soon

After someone had stolen it to replace
One of the horses killed in the battle
Something he justified to his own race
When saying he didn't steal the saddle

A Fourth of July Celebration
58

Bonney stopped at the store in Roswell
While McSween went on to Chisums ranch
And so right here Ash Upton would sell
Him a box of candy hearts on the hunch

They are Sally Chisums favorite sweets
Because William Bonney felt partial to
A blond girl with large bosom or teats
And dreamt about her as lots of men do

Including the three pals who rode next
To him after leaving the general store
Some observer described a hurried exit
After seeing riders of a dozen or more

Suddenly coming along the road to town
And then recognized they were Warriors
Led by Buck Powell banging his six gun
With no tall hills or natural barriers

To halt shots from the posse who raced
Them even as far as John Chisums ranch
Where Bonney gave a warning then faced
Buck Powell and all of that damn bunch

By climbing on the roof and from there
Shooting from behind walls of a façade
Built like a Spanish mission and where
Many of its occupants felt very afraid

Save for Sally Chisum who wouldn't let
This event keep her from doing laundry
Even after the cowboys had taken a bet
She might die and so it was a quandary

For everyone including Bonney who gave
Sally the box of hearts and then asked
That she go inside while she said save
Your breaths sweet boy and then basked

In happiness at Bonney's embarrassment
That showed again why Bonney liked her
Courage and humor like some endearment
And charm that everybody who was there

Couldn't help seeing and which started
The rumor going that both of them were
Sweethearts and for some time thwarted
Strangers from interrupting them there

Some Barbeque Western Style

Then later on that same morning Powell
Saw ranch cowboys coming off the range
And so quickly mounted to get the hell
Away from there due to a sudden change

In the balance of power as the cowboys
Wandered in and ate delicious barbeque
Spicy steaks and ribs everybody enjoys
When black cooks appeared as if on cue

Telling them they missed the fireworks
When the posse guns had filled the air
With smoke about which everybody jokes
Including Sally and Bonney a cute pair

Since they play with Bonneys small dog
The breed called Aztec Chihuahua while
Chico the dog who was a bit of a rogue
Also tried to steal meats off the pile

Where twenty one men seated on benches
Would empty big plates of hot victuals
While sentinels stood at their watches
Searching for an enemy through portals

As leaders sought private celebrations
Stood up and then filed from the table
To some room for serious conversations
With John who gave them the best label

Of whiskey and the finest Cuban cigars
So as to honor the great American flag
That still hung with many battle scars
Over the mantel beside the trophy stag

All because of McSween who needed help
In the struggle for Lincoln and feared
Rightly they would be beaten to a pulp
Unless John Chisums cowboys interfered

But Chisum remained adamant about this
Then said he would not become involved
Even though Dolan and Riley could kiss
His ass and so this left it unresolved

Until McSween with nothing more to say
Suddenly turned ashen or deathly white
While he stood up and then walked away
Feeling amazed Chisum ran from a fight

Bonneys Little Dog Plays Tricks
60

So naturally McSween felt disappointed
With Chisum who had been the president
Of the bank a position McSween pointed
Out to Chisum after he became reticent

And they were ready to leave his ranch
Ostensibly because he was afraid women
There might get hurt if the wild bunch
Should return again to fight their men

When McSween wearing all black clothes
Got on his horse without shaking hands
Because the two of them were like foes
Or opposites since neither understands

The other at that moment when suddenly
Gunshots were heard beyond those walls
When McSween spurred his horse if only
To see what happened and quickly calls

The group of men together where Bonney
Was busy shooting a pistol in the dirt
Which everyone there thought was funny
When the little dog without being hurt

Ran excitedly to catch all the bullets
By leaping and biting at the clouds of
Dust in the air like comedy which lets
The cowboys there experience some love

Shared between all of their companions
Knowing full well in time their battle
Will decide the town and its dominions
When everyone swung up into the saddle

All at once as they heard the voice of
McSween tell everyone to come with him
When he spurred his horse and rode off
Along the road under a cottonwood limb

So that Bonney would hurry to scoop up
The Chihuahua that had run on ahead by
Leaning sideways one boot in a stirrup
Galloping too and got it the first try

Showing skill so impressive O'Folliard
Would make a joke about it and whistle
Saying I dare you to do something hard
Why not train the dog to shoot a rifle

Bonney Helps Martin Chavez

McSween had delayed their move to town
So that Bonney could seek the ranchero
Of Martin Chavez who said with a frown
Some Texans who camped next to Picacho

And its river with some covered wagons
Would not pay a bet when losing a race
To his horse and defended with weapons
The cattle that should be on his place

So that Bonney became angry and wanted
To help Martin after hearing the story
And up on his spirited horse sauntered
Although the gentle women indeed worry

He will be killed if he goes all alone
Down to where the Texans keep the herd
But Billy grins still afraid of no one
And kills one cow a second and a third

Before he lowers that rifle and leaves
And then rides back to the Chavez home
To tell Martin to get the three beeves
That he won which were worth an income

More than most Mexicans made in a year
But this very much angers those Texans
About a dozen cowboys who felt no fear
And went to seek revenge on that man's

Foolishness and met Martin who arrived
With two mules to haul away the steers
And asked who it was so Martin replied
Billy the Kid a name that brings tears

To even the most courageous among them
Since they all heard of his reputation
And know it could be a serious problem
If he came again without an invitation

And since they needed no further proof
Of his nerve they gather up belongings
And put them under a white canvas roof
Before they hitch oxen teams to wagons

And then slowly cross that prairie now
Leaving the beeves behind on the scene
For Martin who rightly won them anyhow
And in gratitude found men for McSween

BOOK THREE

The Five Day Battle Begins

Ella Bolton heard the clatter of boots
On the porch boards and simultaneously
The jingle of spurs and her hair roots
Stood on end when someone ungraciously

Gave a sharp rap on the outside wooden
Door that she hoped latched and locked
Like she always tried to remember when
Her husband was away then felt shocked

When she recognized the voice of Billy
Bonney as he spoke from the other side
And so she jumped from bed willy nilly
To light the lantern and tried to hide

Her bare skin by clutching the clothes
Around her throat as soon as she undid
The latch and then opened to see roses
Now given by the hand of Billy the Kid

In compensation for forcing her out of
The Ellis house which eight Regulators
Occupy even before she takes with love
The offered bouquet of crimson flowers

Near the moment her teen daughter Ella
The same one who had danced with Billy
Had her feet lifted up after the polka
And walked off in a huff feeling silly

Suddenly came from the bedroom to find
The boy staring at her and was told by
Her worried mother not to stray behind
But to dress pronto without saying why

They would leave for the Montano house
At ten at night then suddenly discover
When they got there that it was in use
By Martin Chaves along with many other

Hispanics who had felt enraged by what
The posse did to destroy their village
So that Billy tipped his tall gray hat
And then apologized for another change

When they went out and he led everyone
Across the street over into the Patron
House where Juan lived there all alone
But Ella was all right with a chaperon

The Morning of the First Day

Early morning July fifteenth eighteen
Seventy eight Saturnino Baca came out
Of his house right about when McSween
Looked in the window and gave a shout

Because he saw that Baca was carrying
Food supplies to and from the Torreon
Where deadly enemy had gone in hiding
Deputy Billy Matthews and Deputy Long

Men who would murder him in the blink
Of an eye if they got the opportunity
Which angered McSween who would think
To evict Baca who rented his property

When he sent a note trying to explain
That he must leave here in three days
Or stay behind and suffer bitter pain
At seeing his house ignite in a blaze

Which scared Baca enough to ride nine
Miles to Ft Stanton to see Col Dudley
Who was unable to help but did assign
Lt Appel to go back with Baca quickly

So he could investigate the situation
Which he did by first meeting McSween
Who said he could justify this action
Against Baca for acting as go between

So then the Lieutenant went to appeal
To Deputy Long who said they will bow
Out only under one condition Lt Appel
Return with troops who will not allow

McSween's forces to gain control over
The Torreon a large round adobe tower
And bastion which they seized earlier
In order to keep the balance of power

Which suddenly shifted as he rode out
Of town on his way back to Ft Stanton
When three posses consisting of about
Forty riders that include James Dolan

John Kinney and Jesse Evans and posse
Leaders Marion Turner and Buck Powell
Rushed passed him to leave all horses
In care of the Wortley Hotel's corral

The Afternoon of the First Day

From a window inside the Montano house
Billy Bonney could see the three gangs
Talking to Dolan who had become hoarse
When suddenly he heard the rapid bangs

Of Winchester rifles shoot at McSweens
The U shaped building with adobe walls
Where half a dozen of his good friends
Were trapped inside and so Billy calls

After cupping his mouth for O'Folliard
To follow him along with five Mexicans
As they bend and hurry across the yard
Running the whole time they shoot guns

At the enemy who must keep their heads
Down low and out of sight or be killed
When they venture out and Bonney leads
The way and then ducks behind a shield

That was part of McSween's house where
All of a sudden the rear door opens up
And he sees the proud and sullen stare
Of McSween himself standing with a cup

Of hot coffee in his right hand and in
His left the large black leather Bible
Because McSween was a devout Christian
Who smiled knowing Bonney was reliable

And steadfast and humorous too because
He called McSween Governor the sublime
Title of Tunstalls when a sudden pause
Came and Deputy Long told them a crime

Was committed and that he had warrants
For the arrests of McSween and Big Jim
French and William Bonney who he wants
To appear so they can surrender to him

But received a negative answer instead
When Bonney climbed on top of the roof
And then made his feet dance with lead
While shouting there wasn't much proof

To show them he had done wrong forcing
Deputy Long to scamper into the saloon
Inside of Waverly Hotel after waltzing
Over the street like a Gazette cartoon

The Second Day of the Battle

The next morning some shots were fired
But neither side gained much advantage
So that Dolan out of frustration hired
A rider to carry the Sheriff's message

To Ft Stanton and deliver it in person
To Colonel Dudley who read the request
For the howitzer and sent Pvt Robinson
Back to Lincoln directly from the west

Where the black soldier heard gunshots
And then told Dolan and Sheriff Peppin
Deputies weren't taking practice shots
But meant to shoot him when he rode in

To the place where posses were located
Something that Dolan vehemently denied
Even though recent positions indicated
It was true and Warriors probably lied

In order to blame it on the Regulators
About sixty who held homes in the east
Where he should shell the perpetrators
Even though Robinson had done his best

To explain to Dolan the howitzer could
Not be used due to the Posse Comitatus
Act before he went back again and told
Col Dudley what was the current status

Of the town making the Colonel furious
Over the fact his soldier was fired on
So that he asked for and got a serious
Meeting to discuss problems in Lincoln

With his officers Lt Appel Capt Blaire
And Capt Purington who have permission
To enter Lincoln tomorrow if they dare
In order to carry out an investigation

That shall verify Pvt Robinson's claim
However in what became an afterthought
Col Dudley took a rather different aim
And ordered an old howitzer be brought

In for repairs at the blacksmiths shop
From where it rest on the fort grounds
In an unusable state tied up with rope
Not very far from the flag pole mounds

The Third Day of the Battle

Early that morning Sheriff Peppin came
Up with the idea he could put deputies
In back of the Montano house and climb
Up the hillside by moving behind trees

Until with rifles they could fire down
On top of Regulators and move everyone
From the roofs but this plan was blown
Away by Fernando Herrera who had a gun

Aimed out the window right at the spot
Charlie Crawford would soon standstill
Only to be doubled over after one shot
Had sent three others running downhill

In the hopes of making it in one piece
All the way back to that Wortley Hotel
Where they walk inside the main office
Only to hear the other boys raise hell

Because the committee of five soldiers
Including the officers mentioned above
Have called them a bunch of damn liars
But recant this since they can't prove

Which side tried to shoot Pvt Robinson
After posse members for Sheriff Peppin
Testified albeit using a faulty reason
They were innocent and immediately pin

Blame for the shooting onto Regulators
Whom Captain Blaire forgot to question
As would any fair minded investigators
But joins the side of their opposition

By holding back his military intention
Which the Regulators had misunderstood
The moment Lt Appel and Capt Purington
Were seen with soldiers along the wood

Of the hilltop and believing they were
There to do harm instantly opened fire
From inside of the Montano house where
Chaves claimed it was not their desire

To prevent in anyway the army rescuers
From taking an injured man to hospital
But only to stop one of their pursuers
Whose wound in a few days proved fatal

The Fourth Day of the Battle

Rev Ealy was nervous when he came from
John Tunstalls store with his wife and
Four children and then walked in front
Of everybody who might have had a hand

At shooting Ben Ellis through the neck
Last evening when it was too dangerous
To come out by himself alone and check
On Ben Ellis who lay rather languorous

Until morning when gradually the fight
Ended and enemies would not be so bold
As to shoot a reverent man in daylight
Risking disapproval of the whole world

But must be patient awhile longer even
Wait until Ealy had returned once more
So they can sneak in behind the tavern
And shoot right through the front door

Wounding George Bowers but killing Tom
Cullins when he stood up in the window
Just then and was taken down to a room
In the cellar used for a sanctuary now

While the enemy moved into near houses
Which belonged to three Hispanic women
Who walked because no available horses
Were in the town of Lincoln right then

A distance of some nine miles to reach
The fort and speak in Col Dudley's ear
Several grievances that clearly breach
Civilized standards by creating a fear

So pernicious it now threatens to harm
Women and children the only real proof
Col Dudley needed to set off the alarm
Inside the meeting when under one roof

He and five of his officers will agree
The armys intervention doesn't violate
The Posse Comitatus Act to this degree
They can aid innocents if not too late

Then Col Dudley recalled that howitzer
Still needed fixing and ordered Nelson
An overworked blacksmith to repair her
Even if he needed an all night session

Around Noon of the Fifth Day

Music on the air seemed faint and small
At first but then gradually grew louder
As fifes and drums set the cadence call
For a sergeant major who seemed prouder

Than anyone including the fine officers
Who looked so gallant alongside cavalry
In blue coats and hats and sharp sabers
Because his voice barked at an infantry

Which obeyed his orders when it shortly
Stopped marching halted all of a sudden
Upon the street in front of the Wortley
So Col Dudley could tell Sheriff Peppin

That his soldiers would kill anyone who
Fired their weapons at the Sheriffs men
At any of his soldiers or at anyone who
Tried to violate the women and children

Before marching on down to a vacant lot
Near the Montano house where they march
By without telling McSween who will jot
Down many observations to keep in touch

With the newspapers which he was handed
By a mailman who heard him repeat right
Would triumph even before Dudley landed
In town showing military pomp and might

In the shape of a Gatling gun he points
Directly across the street at the front
Of Montano's house where Cheves squints
From the window and in words very blunt

Tells them all to evacuate the building
Before everyone looks like Swiss cheese
Until this became the reason for hiding
Faces with blankets while they squeezed

Passed building walls and a Gatling gun
Which also threatens at the Ellis house
Where the majority of them went to join
Forces until their situation grew worse

Each minute because of Col Dudleys trap
And all of a sudden shoot their way out
Through Sheriff Peppin's men and escape
On the horses after experiencing a rout

Col Dudley Demands Arrests

It should go without saying Col Dudley
Was mad as hell because Sheriff Peppin
Had let all of the Regulators get away
When army tactics said they should win

Thus forcing Dudley to make a new plan
And without wasting any time he orders
An ailing Justice Wilson to come stand
Before a committee made up of soldiers

Who order him to issue arrest warrants
Because McSween resists Sheriff Peppin
But Wilson abstains until Dudley rants
And threatens to bring the governor in

So that a coerced Justice Wilson signs
The warrant after three officers swear
In affidavit their investigation finds
That Pvt Robinson had justifiable fear

When suddenly fired upon by Regulators
Who were in McSweens when the warrants
Were served by cigar smoking dictators
Men like Marion Turner who soon chants

He has to arrest everyone in the house
But then heard Big Jim French poke fun
Saying they had warrants too of course
Both in paper and in the form of a gun

Asking Turner to go ahead and pick one
Because Turner was the kind of man you
Easily hate for the things he had done
In the past and was now planning to do

At the jail when he used McSween's own
Servants Sebrian and George Washington
And freed them so they could burn down
His house at least the eastern portion

By stacking wood in a pile on the side
He would pour coal oil and then ignite
With a match on the instant Liz Shield
Smelled smoke and rushed upon the site

To douse the flames with water buckets
From a window then scolds the servants
Who jump all about as if stuck piglets
And in the excitement piss their pants

Sue McSween Sees Col Dudley

Until puddles spread around their feet
And the two servants become hysterical
And run away shouting Turner will beat
And kill them unless God's own miracle

Will prevent him and then does because
A man called the Dummy and Deputy Long
Volunteer to do the job and then pause
Hesitate for only moments and yet long

Enough to alert the Regulators who see
They are ready to burn McSween's house
With buckets of coal oil and all agree
They must act now with no time to lose

When instantly from the Tunstall store
The likes of Sam Smith and Henry Brown
And George Coe begin to fire and score
A victory in that these men throw down

The buckets and then jump in the privy
In McSween's back yard lifting the lid
Up to inhale fetid odors like a livery
Until their sickened faces look pallid

When they cover themselves in the muck
To avoid getting hit by flying bullets
And lie in a hole where they will duck
Their heads and spend hours of regrets

Waiting there while Sue McSween crawls
On the ground upon her hands and knees
But stands up at the Torreon and bawls
At Sheriff Peppin with whom she pleads

Even demands to know why he forced her
Two servants into burning her new home
To which Peppin said did it ever occur
To you we would stop if you were alone

So that Sue had no choice but to enter
The camp of Col Dudley then ask why he
Did not protect herself and her sister
Who had five children and he said they

Would not help Sue McSween because she
Harbored the likes of Billy Bonney and
Big Jim French a problem she would see
As not only unfair but mostly partisan

An Interlude in C Sharp Minor

Sue McSween her voice strident in tone
Quarreled with Col Dudley for whom she
Felt no respect since he deserved none
Until she upset the Colonel so much he

Told her to leave at once his big tent
And then threatened to call his guards
To throw her out if she wasn't content
Using her own volition since the barbs

Cut his pride and so she had no choice
But to turn an about face and walk out
Of the army tent he used for an office
To head home and leave the offish lout

Which was what she called him and more
Unflattering words that she never told
Her husband who hugged Sue by the door
And said Martin Cheves once again held

The height with the help of Regulators
Who had returned to make a final stand
On the hill at least until the terrors
Of the Gatling gun aimed and fired and

They again had to make a hasty retreat
Leaving what was an unbearable silence
In the room where she slid on the seat
Of her prized piano and would commence

To play a song that fit her melancholy
And reminded her of much happier times
Of holidays when she played hymns holy
For Bonney and O'Folliard whose crimes

Committed were they sang like amateurs
And laughed aloud with baritone voices
Until completely possessed of seizures
Sue ceased by making discordant noises

On the piano ivory because she smelled
A pungent and acrid smoke from the air
And was shocked when Andy Boyle yelled
To others he had set the house on fire

By igniting kindling on the windowsill
While fanning the flame with coal oils
Until the roof caught ablaze and still
Burned irregardless of everyones toils

A Sudden Evacuation Begins

The explosion stunned all who heard it
Including Col Dudley who believed that
Someone had fired the howitzer without
His express orders and immediately sat

Out on his horse to reprimand the unit
Responsible and so was quite surprised
To learn black gunpowder had caused it
When the small keg in the house raised

Sections of the red tiled roof exactly
When a stunned and fearful Susan Gates
A school teacher who sat with Rev Ealy
And his family of five quickly debates

Within herself whether she is a coward
Or not and then suddenly walks outside
To where Col Dudley meets with a crowd
Of observers and swallowing hurt pride

Demands the protection of some escorts
Which he grants and comes with a wagon
That takes Ealys family too and starts
For the house belonging to Juan Patron

And since the wagon goes directly past
McSween's house this gave both sisters
Sue and Liz sudden opportunity at last
To run out and join with the resistors

Who were leaving the tumultuous battle
At around two o'clock in the afternoon
When the group of drunken men belittle
The ladies by promising they will soon

Kill all of the boys left in the house
Either by their bullets or by barbeque
Since the roof burned like a slow fuse
And Dudley's military refused a rescue

Dooming them to inevitable destruction
If all of the Regulators stayed inside
Thoughts that so depressed Ella Bolton
Billys dance partner she quickly cried

While looking up at the cloud of smoke
That rose up in the air like a chimney
Above the town because her heart awoke
Whispering she was in love with Bonney

McSween Murdered by Enemies

Nobody said what would happen but they
Knew McSween must come out in the open
At a time when everyone would be ready
The exact moment when they were broken

When one room was burnt and men inside
Ran to the next room and then the next
Until the only place anyone could hide
Was the kitchen the last place of exit

From where the Mexicans enter the yard
Looking exposed in the light of flames
Where McSween came with Tom O'Folliard
And Billy Bonney and Bob Beckwith aims

From behind that small perimeter fence
Where his deputies are hiding and then
Shoots Alex McSween to end the silence
That erupts with gunshots all a sudden

Bob Beckwith's hitting McSweens breast
Killing him instantly the exact moment
Bonney saw a flame where his hand rest
Pulled the trigger at his hip and sent

A bullet up his wrist and into his eye
Ending Beckwith's life before he turns
Round and then will unsuccessfully try
To steady McSween when the house burns

And all of a sudden the roof top falls
Then Regulators fly in every direction
As Bonney shoots along four foot walls
To keep their heads down and shall run

Not to seek safety in the near shelter
A chicken coop where Zamora and Romero
In panic hide and frighten the rooster
And hens and immediately become a hero

Sharing three and eight bullets apiece
Nor with Salazar who falls in the yard
Shot in the back on a roll of the dice
But gambling his life on the wild card

He joins Gonzales and Sanchez who were
Running around the corner of the house
In an attempt to escape Deputies there
A situation that would soon grow worse

How Some Regulators Escape

Although it was nine oclock pitch dark
Save for flames beating back the night
There was no moon and only a dogs bark
Sounding almost frantic when the fight

Had immediately moved to the back yard
Behind the burned house where Deputies
Looked to see with eyes straining hard
Unusual movement within the subtleties

That abound in shadow where Regulators
By this time had reached the back gate
Before being surprised by the Warriors
Who sprang from where they lay in wait

And suddenly gunned down Harvey Morris
A law student boarding at the McSweens
Who lived there since his tuberculosis
Required dry air or a change of scenes

When his doctor recommended New Mexico
And specifically Lincoln never a place
Where Harvey thought anyone would blow
His head off after surviving a furnace

Just before he fell dead on the ground
And made the others leap over his body
As they ran through the gate and bound
Away like deer when Bonney shot Kinney

And wounds his cheek just as he sneaks
Round one of the corners to shoot once
More at the Regulators or rather peaks
Around the corner looking like a dunce

When the skills and marksmanship which
Bonney had tried to teach Harvey found
Its mark with words you son of a bitch
Predicating John Kinneys howling sound

One second before Billy hurled himself
Across that gate and was soon followed
By O'Folliard who had become very deft
At aiding others but this time allowed

His instincts to run off into the wood
With Harveys gun and quickly disappear
In the bush where everybody understood
He lingered behind to cover their rear

George Coes Fabulous Dream

When the three men heard more shooting
Going on outside of the Tunstall store
They foresaw the Regulators evacuating
Then tried to escape out the back door

By climbing up over the eightfoot wall
Using some of the empty wooden barrels
Like a platform and then dangling fall
On the other side where tall chaparral

Bushes grew up beside the Bonito River
On whose banks flow that gentle stream
During a night their flesh will shiver
And George Coe will experience a dream

After following a path that takes them
Behind the Ellis House where Uncle Ike
Sees their presence there as a problem
And instantly tells them to leave like

It or not because their own lives were
At risk if this enemy should ever know
Sam Corbet gave George his hat to wear
Or Aunt Nancy one of his kin should go

Fetch bread and smoked ham for lunches
From a cupboard that she also searches
For dessert and discovers ripe peaches
Which they ate after everybody reaches

The mountain top overlooking that town
Where upwards rose like a phoenix bird
On soft velvet night the splendid moon
That softly whispered without any word

Suspending briefly the nights intrigue
That weighed heavily on men lying back
Their droopy eyelids closed by fatigue
When a conscious George Coe will track

A round moon whose archery like motion
Rose high above the earth's dark abyss
And enchantment emptied him of emotion
So he fell asleep and awoke with bliss

When the day dawned on a new beginning
And during an epiphany he was set free
Of all old hatreds and started walking
To find a small choza that sold coffee

Black Fiddlers Dance of Death

While McSween lay dead out in the yard
His left hand clutching the Holy Bible
That he worshipped as the one true God
Crowds of looters robbed like a rabble

The Tunstall store of stocks of liquor
Going back for more bullets and cigars
Even all of the donations for the poor
Lifting coins out of broken glass jars

Shameful acts that made black servants
Disregard their safety in an apartment
Where they lived to object amid taunts
Of nigger from drunken men who torment

Sons of slaves by forcing them outside
To make music for cruel macabre dances
Playing fiddles and bows as they cried
Seated on the wall by averting glances

Just as Andy Boyle ran McSween through
With lead making him pay for his crime
Then went over to do the same thing to
Yginio Salazar who in the nick of time

Was spared from death when Milo Pierce
Told Boyle that he was damn disgusting
And then because Milo looked so fierce
Boyle held onto the pistol not cocking

The hammer or wanting to shoot Salazar
Who simply play dead the whole time he
Lay prone there motionless in the yard
Not flinching until it was about three

In the morning when the noisy revelers
Had all gone off to bed and passed out
Not to awaken for hours with travelers
When he feels safe and crawls in front

Of the bridge where it meets the river
Down on his stomach and upright stands
To wander under his own unsteady power
For about half a mile until both hands

Now closed in a fist pound on the door
Belonging to his sister in law's house
Who opens to see him fall on the floor
Where he makes a bad injury even worse

Three Deputies Come for Salazar

Early next morning Col Dudley examined
The battle field from the night before
Along with Lt Dan Appel who determined
Precise cause of death and furthermore

Gave some assistance to the undertaker
John Newcomb when he came in the wagon
For the deceased and saw Marion Turner
And John Kinney and Andy Boyle come on

The scene after they had been stealing
From Tunstall's store and noticed that
Andy Boyle now stood up there pointing
At the spot where Yginio Salazar's hat

Lay on the ground looking at the trail
Of blood they immediately shall follow
Where it leads to Salazar without fail
Unless Dr Appel prevented them somehow

Since he knew Salazar was at the house
Where he had just spent half the night
Replacing bandages and spooning a dose
Of elixir for wounds made in the fight

Because Appel suspected such movements
And told Dudley he must return to camp
To find a forgotten bag of instruments
Also a horse that would friskily stamp

When he mounted and rode in the saddle
Covering the half a mile in good speed
Up to the house where he would startle
The three men caught right in the deed

Of carrying Salazars body out the door
So that as he shouted for them to stop
They dropped Salazar down on the floor
Then yelled like an Indian would whoop

Because he said he would see them hang
If Salazar died from the loss of blood
Saving the boy from a most brutal gang
While a hysterical sister in law stood

In a night gown and screamed murderers
As Appel took his body in light of day
Back inside the house by his shoulders
While the three abductors slipped away

McSweens Wife Vows Revenge

During a two day aftermath Sue McSween
Came out from where she was staying at
Juan Patrons so that she could be seen
By many townspeople who in windows sat

Like immobile stones to gape and stare
When she walked along that main street
With Ella Bolton and snubbed the glare
That felt victorious within her defeat

To observe her house that lay in ruins
And ashes while pushing back the tears
Since the only thing left were strings
Where her beloved St Louis piano sears

In the hot coals in which she dug with
Ends of a long pole to find the locket
With her husbands image that was worth
More money than she held in her pocket

And which she would keep in her drawer
Then kiss with her lips before falling
Asleep every night uttering the prayer
And that same promise she made calling

Out his name over and over again aloud
As if though Alex could hear her words
Even from that graveyard where a crowd
Of soldiers had buried him with swords

Dangling from their sides right behind
The store where John Tunstall was laid
To rest making her think she was blind
Not to have done this without more aid

Until in a bright flash she understood
It didn't matter how many fighters sat
Inside the house then Col Dudley would
Have acted the same way no matter what

So then vowed over her husband's grave
While the crowd was curiously watching
With the knowledge she had acted brave
To complete that plan she was hatching

In her brain vengeance and retribution
At Col Dudley who must share the blame
In court for her husband's destruction
If she was to clear the McSween's name

An Enemy Calls on Sue McSween

When Jack Easton overseer of the House
Passed the Tunstall store and then saw
Mexicans steal from it he felt remorse
For Sue McSween and for what civil law

Had done and so waited inside Patron's
Seated patiently in the room adjoining
Where the perfume scented ladies gowns
Decorated the atmosphere with stunning

Patterns when a black man would escort
Him in the parlor where Sue was seated
And then received Jack Easton's report
Which became a reasoned if over heated

Argument that described those Mexicans
As a big party of villains and thieves
Hardly any better than the red Indians
When hiding merchandize up the sleeves

Or in their blankets and who currently
Were stealing items in bright daylight
And would continue till she diligently
Stopped it and made the building tight

Again by nailing boards on the windows
They had broken and so who could blame
Easton for being mad after the widow's
Response seemed so contrary and insane

When she agreed with what had happened
Then said the poor can take everything
Because the store shall be left opened
Since none was there to guard anything

And that it was better the poor should
Have it than the Sheriffs Deputies who
Had taken much stuff already and would
Not pay for it making them thieves too

So Jack Easton was shocked by the time
That he left there then went back home
To mediate and think about the sublime
Irony which the Lincoln War had become

In just a year's time after the deaths
Of McSween and Tunstall and the others
Brady and Hindmann too since in earths
Graves all men at last lie as brothers

Bonney Hides From Sheriff Peppin

After Abram Miller heard a quick knock
He opened up the peep hole just enough
In the front door to make a tiny crack
And was glad to see Bonney not a tough

Hombre who waited outside on the steps
While Abram negotiated with his mother
For three minutes but who then accepts
The fact Billy had fought on the other

Side with McSween and that she was not
In danger just because she knew Murphy
On whose ranch Abram cow punched a lot
Mostly because his mother needed money

And then too since Billy had been kind
To Abram last year when the Regulators
Visited Elk Canyon camp hoping to find
John Tunstall's murderous perpetrators

And so Billy ate a hearty supper there
And then stayed all the night and next
Morning when he and Abram became aware
Of a posse stopping and on the pretext

Of milking cows Abram visited a corral
Where there was a fine horse all black
In color so Sheriff Peppin would drawl
Asking why it had a saddle on its back

Until he grew suspicious so that three
Deputies were told to search the house
Thoroughly and yet no one ever did see
A padlocked trunk his mother would use

To hide Billy from a posse that leaves
Soon after to continue along the trail
While a very much relieved Billy stays
Behind one more night and without fail

Next day asks Abram if he could borrow
His fine black horse to flee the posse
And this much to Abram Miller's sorrow
Since he thinks that he will never see

The fine horse he had traded an Indian
For beads and red cloth and gun powder
But Abram found it in the corral again
For Billy returned it a few days later

Martinez Kills Morris Bernstein

Over the next few days more Regulators
Began to arrive at San Patricio either
Coming on foot with blisters and sores
Or riding mounts all in a heavy lather

From trying to outrun sheriff's posses
Until a business meeting made it clear
They needed to replace the many horses
Lost in town at the Lincoln County War

Which they manage to acquire by buying
And borrowing and last resort stealing
From ranchers they believe to be lying
Like Madame Casey punished for dealing

With their hated foes but because they
Fall short of the goal they all remedy
The situation by going many miles away
To visit the Apache Reservation Agency

That was located beside Blazer's Mills
Where everyone recalled that same year
The battle where Buckshot Rogers kills
Dick Brewer whose graves lay very near

The corrals of the Indian Agency where
Morris Bernstein a clerk for the store
Who was giving rations to squaws there
Heard gunshots then knew it meant more

Horse thieves and so picked up a rifle
And then rode straight into the battle
Where Indian and Mexican shots whistle
Then knock him clear out of the saddle

By a freshwater spring where Constable
Martinez told the Regulators afterward
He killed Bernstein before he was able
To harm the boys who stood in the yard

Watering their horses that suddenly go
Leaving behind men like Bonney to jump
In a saddle right up behind George Coe
Who let the others control the roundup

While they rode to higher ground above
Arriving as they opened up that corral
To lasso agency horses they then drove
Down to the bottom land with chaparral

All the Regulators Bid Farewell
82

So the Regulators arrived at Ft Sumner
An old army post owned by Pete Maxwell
And soon spend money like it was water
Since after a few days they could sell

Half of the herd to the local Mexicans
Who were glad to find good horse flesh
At low prices without asking questions
Just so long as they could pay in cash

Which they spend in one of two saloons
Where girls with long hair sport roses
Above earrings made from silver spoons
And also smell lots better than horses

Until they pull up roots and go beyond
To the next town but not everyone goes
Some of the Regulators plan to stay on
Scurlock and Bowdre who take the wives

With belongings from the Ruidoso ranch
To settle at Ft Sumner where they find
Work on the Maxwell or the Yerby ranch
Where the Regulators leave them behind

To further seek their fortune in towns
Such as Puerto De Luna and Anton Chico
Where George Coe collects a few frowns
By saying he and his brother Frank Coe

Were leaving that day for the Sugareet
Which made more want to depart as well
So that Regulators numbered only eight
When they shook hands and bid farewell

To those who followed Bonney on a raid
Right straight back to enemy territory
For more horses they find at the Fritz
Ranch and sell in Tascosa as the story

Goes the very last horse to Henry Hoyt
A young doctor adventuring in the West
Who took Dandy Dick without knowing it
Belonged to Sheriff Brady for the best

Part of a year before somebody pointed
Out to him that the Arabian sorrel was
Indeed the same horse the sheriff used
Somber news that made the doctor pause

A Special Agent Reports Corruption

A few months prior to this Frank Angel
Visited Lincoln wanting to investigate
Various reasons why people would rebel
Against territorial laws he would rate

Poorly ministered by corrupt officials
In his report to Secretary of Interior
Carl Schurz who coauthors and initials
A letter he would send to his superior

President Hayes who without hesitation
Removed that largest obstacle to peace
Gov Axtell from his new administration
Replacing him with General Lew Wallace

Whose first solemn duty was to request
From the Generals Sherman and Sheridan
Permission for marshal law in the West
Yet these two men failed to understand

The situation and when they had denied
That request Governor Wallace appealed
To both warring factions as he applied
Rules of amnesty hoping that it healed

Everyone who had taken part and fought
In the Lincoln County War except those
Holding previous indictments who ought
To have a jury trial as everyone knows

Men like Peppin who quit being Sheriff
To become a meat butcher at Ft Stanton
Because his very life was in danger if
Col Dudley refused to offer protection

To civilians who feared Selman Raiders
And stayed at the fort because anarchy
Spread throughout due to the soldier's
Inability to defend farms and property

From the marauders who would even rape
Women who were left on the farms alone
Doing violence which none could escape
Even before showing he would not atone

Col Dudley declared Lincoln off limits
For soldiers stationed at Fort Stanton
And barred all refuges without permits
Thus sealing their doom by this action

Lawyer Chapman Helps McSween

Huston Chapman a lawyer from Las Vegas
Was hired by Sue McSween to defend her
Rights in court against the very bogus
Rumors aimed at smearing her character

Which at least according to Col Dudley
Was like a loose woman coarse and lewd
During a meeting when she could hardly
Stand up from being too drunk and rude

A skewed opinion that he had and wrote
About in a letter sent to the Governor
In Santa Fe who frequently would quote
From it and show Col Dudley more favor

The very reason that lawyer would call
One day with David Shields her brother
In law who got her buggy and drove all
The way to Santa Fe in order to badger

The new Governor into letting him read
The letter he would submit as evidence
To the courts unless Col Dudley agreed
To apologize for his strong repugnance

A request that Governor Wallace denied
Saying that he wanted to visit Lincoln
To see for himself if the Colonel lied
About Mrs McSween and also James Dolan

Who the Colonel defended in his letter
Submitting the compromise that Chapman
Brought back to Lincoln a little later
Hoping to himself Sue would understand

When he got there instead of being hot
When to his big surprise she asked him
To stay for supper and made him a spot
At the table and said at least a crime

Had been solved after Sheriff Kimbrell
Arrested the men who had stolen cattle
From Tunstall's herd a gang he'd quell
After surprising them without a battle

An apt situation that nicely coincided
On her being appointed executor of all
Estates since Alex's will had included
Those of Dick Brewer and John Tunstall

Two Rival Gangs Ask for Peace

Though Bonney had previous indictments
That denied him amnesty reconciliation
Was in the air to forget old arguments
That had spawned murder and litigation

So Bonney taking advantage of the time
Wrote a letter to his enemy Jess Evans
At Fort Stanton who agreed to meet him
And four of his good Regulator friends

Behind the Wortley Hotel in the corral
On February 18th eighteen seventy nine
Just a year from the death of Tunstall
When suddenly Jess stepped out of line

Then acting like a betrayer would call
On them to murder Bonney when they had
Him there his back up against the wall
And yet the Kid wasn't afraid and said

He'd kill whoever fired the first shot
Even though he was put down afterwards
Starting an argument that grew red hot
Like a gambler found cheating at cards

And in this way both groups carried on
Until somebody came forward Edgar Walz
Recent brother in law to Thomas Catron
And in movements like a two step waltz

Suggests ending the Lincoln County War
To put away their guns and shake hands
So they could be friends and never mar
One more day of peace by taking stands

On opposite sides and with this advice
They follow Edgar Walz into the saloon
Where he would encourage if not entice
Both parties to sit and drink and soon

Draft a treaty on which they all could
Agree and then swear with raised glass
None would testify in court none would
Ambush each other or talk to the Press

Since they could expect imminent death
To happen at anytime from these others
An oath they spoke with drunken breath
While leaving arm in arm like brothers

Huston Chapman Dies Like a Hero

While they cross the street at Patrons
They are met by the two black servants
Who move about with George Washingtons
Old bear rifle to silence their taunts

Just long enough so Sebrian can inform
Walz that Mrs McSween was busy tonight
When the guest Juan Patron shall storm
Suddenly by the guards to miss a fight

With the men by quickly running inside
On his way to eat with McSween and her
Lawyer Huston Chapman who would reside
At Tunstalls room where he sets a fire

In the stove because the night is cold
And who shall due to the circumstances
Upon his return meet the drunken crowd
Who with guns out makes sure he dances

Shoots at his feet hoping he goes home
Because they don't want him in Lincoln
But Chapman like a man crying for doom
Recklessly said he would do all he can

To send them to the gallows for murder
At the very same moment Billy Campbell
Removed a pistol and then made thunder
Although no rain was in the sky at all

Causing lawyer Chapman to grasp at his
Stomach and then stumble over sideways
With the word murder still on his lips
When Jesse Evans calm as a pickle says

He wants to check out the Oyster House
And insists that Regulators come along
To join the gang while Chapmans blouse
Catches fire and burns because the gun

Had exploded near it with a sound that
Sue McSween heard and knew immediately
Without leaving her room some damn rat
Murdered him as a favor for Col Dudley

Who later dismissed a Coroner's report
That confirmed alcohol had been poured
Over his body in quantities of a quart
Leaving his flesh blackened and scored

The Regulators Feel Betrayed

Quickly feeling betrayed and surprised
That Jesse Evans gang would shoot down
The one armed lawyer they all realized
They urgently needed to leave the town

Before the law found them at McCulluns
Where Walz was worried because Chapman
He now learned wasn't wearing any guns
A story they can read on the newsstand

He said as they ate oysters in a house
Of the Pacific variety gotten from God
Knows where just when a stream of ooze
Soiled the chin of Evans who would nod

And flush the food with great swallows
Of frothy beer after he solemnly began
A speech to save them from the gallows
By placing a second pistol in his hand

Claiming he was killed in self defense
After he shot at Dolan from the street
A crafty plan that made a lot of sense
To the room full of gamblers who cheat

By stacking up the odds against Bonney
When Evans handed him that same pistol
That he wanted laid near Chapmans body
And said do precisely what he was told

Or else risk breaking their new treaty
Which was dead as soon as Chapman died
At least to Billy who with palm sweaty
Took hold off the pistol and then lied

Saying it was time they leave the town
That they'll do the job on the way out
Words said in anger making Evans frown
And everyone look as Evans would shout

He'd send Campbell along for a witness
Since he only wanted to see if the Kid
Would do what he was told because Jess
Was jealous and of course he never did

For as soon as Bonney had gone outside
He gave the pistol to Campbell instead
Telling him that he had too much pride
And without lingering hurried on ahead

Sheriff Kimbrell Looks for Killers

It stands to reason then Billy the Kid
A boy that everyone knew by reputation
Would be the first criminal they tried
To arrest along with his one companion

Tom O'Folliard on account of prejudice
People have when the facts are unknown
And judge with criticism until justice
Triumphs and in the end truth is shown

Which was the very reason why the army
Under Lt Goodwin departed Fort Stanton
With orders to try and restore harmony
To Lincoln where indeed there was none

And went to San Patricio on request of
Sheriff Kimbrell to arrest the two men
For Chapman's murder but without proof
And soon discovered that every citizen

Swore loyalty to the Regulators and so
Felt disappointed at leaving the scene
For Thomas Catron's ranch at Carrizozo
Because they heard that Evans had been

Hiding there with the rest of his gang
And arrested them for Chapman's murder
A crime for which they should all hang
According to Sue McSweens hired lawyer

Ira Leonard who recently filed charges
That would hold Col Dudley responsible
For the death of McSween and he argues
Ruined the house since it was possible

To save the roof by dousing the flames
If he had acted to form a fire brigade
With pails of water and rightly blames
Col Dudley comparing him to a renegade

For not letting soldiers restore order
And then wrote so many damning letters
Governor Wallace would start to wonder
If he ought to look into these matters

And then deciding that he'd had enough
He sent Gen Hatch to remove Col Dudley
From the post of commander even though
That officer requested to stay on duty

Bonney Meets Governor Wallace

On March 17th Bonney rode into Lincoln
Under the cover of darkness along with
Two compadres who heard Justice Wilson
Say that spoken rumors were not a myth

Gov Wallace was in his house right now
But he only wanted to see Billy Bonney
And that for safety he could not allow
Things they had brought on the journey

Weapons that Bonney handed over to his
Friend Tom O'Folliard who remained out
In the hall by Doc Scurlock while this
Late hour meeting began within earshot

Of them while Justice Wilson was there
To take down notes and read the letter
Bonney wrote to make Gov Wallace aware
That they wanted to make things better

By coming to testify against Chapman's
Murderers in exchange for full amnesty
Which Wallace promised and shook hands
To convey a sense of trust and honesty

And said he would arrange for them all
To leave San Patricio under the escort
Of a posse trained by Sheriff Kimbrell
Who had agreed by means of last resort

To let the fighters hold their weapons
Anywhere in town except the courthouse
Just so long as they stayed in Patrons
Did not damage property or break loose

From the place of confinement all this
Because Billy told Wallace they needed
Protection from what was a final twist
In a plot that was further complicated

By the assassins who can night and day
Stop the mouths belonging to witnesses
Then prevent whatever they want to say
Like when Bonney to the jury confesses

What it was like to see Huston Chapman
Collapse all of a sudden on the ground
After Campbell shot him with a six gun
And his shirt caught fire from a round

The Conclusions of the Court
Part I

Since both courts took so long to hear
The testimony given by each eyewitness
And long delays built tension and fear
Many found ways to reduce their stress

For example Bonney and friends staying
At Patron's enjoyed music from guitars
And violins during sunset each evening
As they drank tequila or smoked cigars

Compliments of a Mexican militia force
Known as Lincoln County Mounted Rifles
All former Regulators hired by Wallace
To keep the peace even though it riles

The enemy when they see so many guests
Before the windows ready to sing songs
For all the prisoners who will request
Titles in Spanish then talk to throngs

Tomorrow when they gather at the court
Saying in English Dudley told the army
Privates at least three times to treat
Those in the McSween house as an enemy

For they wanted to inflict bodily harm
And this gone undisputed by Col Dudley
Who said with a stiff regimented charm
He ordered his troops to return volley

If fired upon and so went the military
Inquiry whose officers were very loyal
To Col Dudley and largely conciliatory
Often treating him like a prince royal

On that day his lawyers would subpoena
Sue McSween who walked inside the door
Looking fragile like a porcelain china
Doll when she briefly hesitated before

Walking down an aisle of the courtroom
A crowd watching as she took her place
A dark veil hiding her eyes from gloom
As she glanced at her adversaries face

And without a change in her expression
Heard that judge say he was not guilty
Of murder or of arson during a session
She languished from the utter futility

The Conclusions of the Court
Part II

When the military trial ended in favor
Of Col Dudley the civilian trial began
With what some believed was good humor
After the court discovered Jesse Evans

Along with Billy Campbell the murderer
Of Huston Chapman had broken from jail
When they jumped a guard on duty there
With Texas Jack and then hit the trail

A situation that then caused the court
To try the leaders of the Warriors for
The murder of MacNab who were in short
Found guilty of this hate crime before

That court moved to dismiss them under
Amnesty rules because none of them had
Pending indictments a grievous blunder
And one that appeared increasingly mad

When the lawyers made a wrong decision
By not trying anyone for the murder of
McSween because by their own admission
A murderous intent could not be proved

Since Bob Beckwith had already expired
Having been killed in the line of duty
And thus excused James Dolan who hired
And befriended the Warriors and Deputy

Marion Turner who were all excused too
For fighting in the Lincoln County War
Until the court had nothing left to do
Except try Billy for shooting the star

Of Sheriff Brady on a prior indictment
An unpardonable thing by amnesty rules
Which instantly filled with excitement
The whole courtroom and too made fools

Out of the Regulators because Rynerson
Requested and was granted Billys trial
Be moved to Dona Ana County the reason
Being that the prosecutor believed all

Of those jurors in the town of Lincoln
Would acquit him on charges for murder
Since they saw him as a hero even then
And had refused that he be taken under

The Regulators Free Billy Bonney

After that Bonney was taken handcuffed
And under guard to Patrons where later
On that evening Tom O'Folliard bluffed
The guard saying he had a small matter

To discuss and then pulled out his gun
Just as Dr Scurlock appeared to disarm
The Deputy of his weapon and then spun
Him around and said they wouldn't harm

The Deputy if he would unlock the door
Which he did since he felt afraid then
And knew he could not stop them before
Other guards were able to join the men

As they freed Bonney then went outside
Where seven friends were waiting there
With horses that they immediately ride
Through Lincoln soon heading somewhere

Nobody knew exactly where but could be
George Coes ranch that savage Warriors
Had ransacked from spite soon after he
Left Lincoln County hating those liars

Who were given pardons through amnesty
Everyone that was except Billy the Kid
Who accepted it like all such travesty
With much cheerful banter since it did

No one good to feel depressed about it
In the same way that George Coe bought
A big new thresher but couldn't use it
So loaned it to a man who never fought

In Lincoln County where William Bonney
Had been only a ranch hand of Tunstall
Then due to events not the least funny
He had become a scapegoat for them all

And by leaving justice became a wanted
Outlaw who had to hide out for a spell
Unable to settle because always hunted
His life now turned into a living hell

If he stayed too long in Lincoln which
The town had named after the President
And would from small La Placida switch
Right after the assassination incident

BOOK FOUR

Rob Widenmann Sails to England

Rob Widenmann could hardly believe all
That happened within a few short years
since his friends McSween and Tunstall
Were dead and he shed a thousand tears

Beginning after their significant loss
From the first day they dined together
At the Exchange Hotel until green moss
Had grown over their gravestones there

And they had left Santa Fe for Lincoln
In the same wagon after McSween parted
Company on the business trip for Dolan
At the time destiny remained uncharted

Before that battle over life insurance
Ended in tragedy and became the reason
He sailed to England to give assurance
To John Tunstall Senior whose only son

Would never return home because he was
Killed by barbarians in a foreign land
Leaving the father baffled by the laws
Of people that he could not understand

Since his son had tried to be cautious
While in Canada and then San Francisco
He not realizing at the time a jealous
Mixture of violent men would bring woe

Inside the door of his stately mansion
Where a young and slow talking Marshal
Rob Widenmann exhibited tender passion
Sailing the ocean to deliver a special

Message plus a wooden chest of clothes
That had belonged to his son till even
He was surprised by the truth of those
Sad hound like eyes when Rob was given

Power of attorney and would eventually
Sell the store in what was the biggest
Irony ever heard by townspeople really
Since it was bought by Dolan who least

Deserved it and this coming from folks
Who'd heard it all until Rynerson buys
Tunstalls Ranch and causes dirty jokes
To spread over town thicker than flies

Lucien Maxwell Buys Fort Sumner

By the time Lucien Maxwell had retired
To the former army camp of Fort Sumner
He was a rich rancher who had inspired
Kit Carson a good friend when a hunter

In John Fremonts expedition to explore
Mountains and deserts of Americas West
Where at the end of life he owned more
Land than most and was put to the test

By then Attorney General Thomas Catron
Who defended his partner's false deeds
To claim certain acres they didn't own
Not because they wanted to clear weeds

But because Lucien had discovered gold
On Baldy Mountain and so Elizabethtown
Was created where miners young and old
Leased land from Maxwell who had grown

Wealthier by far selling mine supplies
Until courts began to choke his throat
And he grew tired of litigation's lies
Wanting peace and quiet and so got out

When he sold more than one million and
A half acres still the largest holding
By anyone in the United States on land
Which his wife had inherited she being

Mexican with ties to the old secretary
Who worked with the Governor of Mexico
Miranda was his name a soul less scary
Than that Santa Fe Ring which would do

Just about anything around that region
To remain in power and became a secret
Republicans group led by Thomas Catron
Whom Bonney would later come to regret

Not having killed since he had advised
Rynerson to give his case to the court
Instead of amnesty making him despised
By lawmen everywhere who would distort

His reputation and bad it all the more
Until Ft Sumner became a little heaven
Although Lucien died five years before
The Maxwell family gave him safe haven

Bonney Shoots to Kill Joe Grant

Billy the Kid's fame continued to grow
Even more after the Lincoln County War
When folks heard he had tried to throw
A William Rynerson out of business for

Having bought Tunstall's old Rio Feliz
Right after Sue McSween lost the ranch
To unpaid taxes which he soon realized
The town sold to save Rynerson a bunch

Of money the same Rynerson who refused
To drop murder charges and let Wallace
Grant Bonney a pardon in that confused
Anarchic amnesty spread over the place

And given to everyone but him it seems
The reason why he liked safe Ft Sumner
And passed these days between extremes
Of being either a rustler or a gambler

Who often would exhibit feats of skill
While shooting targets with his pistol
Taking challenges from anyone who will
Pay up in costly cartridges or alcohol

While always being alert for strangers
Like Joe Grant who fails each match up
At target shooting and suddenly angers
Later on after he fills everyone's cup

Inside Teets saloon with Irish whiskey
Telling everyone his name is Texas Red
Boasting he can draw blood from Bonney
By getting off the first piece of lead

He being faster and in a reckless dare
Would prove it with hand on the handle
Of his gun as seen by eyewitness there
Frank Loyed when Billy drew his pistol

After saying I'll go you and then shot
Three times shooting Grant in the chin
And mouth and neck while he was caught
With his hand on the handle all within

A split second he changing from benign
Friend to somebody who frightened them
Giving those near the bar a clear sign
Bullies like Joe Grant were no problem

The Town Gossips About Bonney

For weeks the townspeople talked about
The Killing of Joe Grant in the saloon
By Billy the Kid who was wearing a hat
The sugar loaf sombrero or five gallon

Besides a nickel plated Colt Thunderer
That had a forty one caliber cartridge
Being the first double action revolver
With ivory handles giving him the edge

Along with excellent marksmanship over
Men like Joe Grant who continue to use
The larger Colt single action revolver
Whose forty five caliber he did choose

Because it made a larger hole in a man
Since one shot could stop anybody dead
In their tracks right where they stand
The reason why Billy shot for the head

Or heart doing it at least three times
Using his brain to out smart Joe Grant
Who showed malicious intent for crimes
During the height of his rave and rant

When liquor impaired his cool judgment
Or sobriety and then removed any sense
He had to avoid the dangerous argument
Because his mind felt dulled and dense

Since he should've known Billy the Kid
Famous for courage would not back down
From a challenge to fight and then did
When the golden haired sometimes brown

Skinned baby blue eyed boy spun around
To quickly kill Joe Grant who everyone
Said deserved it and the Justice found
Witnesses saying nothing could be done

Making his services not needed anymore
After exonerating Billy on the charges
Of murder which town women talked more
About than the men and said young ages

Get wrong ideas and might even look up
To Billy as was in the case of Paulita
Maxwell whose brother told her to stop
Inviting Billy to the house for fiesta

Bonney Wants to Kill John Chisum

Late one afternoon inside Teets saloon
As Bonney sat at a table playing cards
With his friends he looked up and soon
Saw John Chisum passing four shepherds

On his way in to eat a meal for supper
Since he had just arrived on the stage
That stopped out front sooner or later
Then seeing the man about sixty in age

Bonny stood up and then left the table
Where he was steadily losing his money
And so walked over to speak or grumble
Over John Chisum who still owed Bonney

Five hundred dollars for past services
In the Lincoln County War which Chisum
Vehemently denied as he quickly spices
His steak and gravy while looking glum

All the while as Bonney went on to say
Yes you do because MacNab had promised
The Regulators then that you would pay
This amount that you later compromised

By not helping either of your partners
For whom I speak because both are dead
And MacNab too making all three goners
Who'd be alive if you'd used your head

To meditate instead of only for eating
And all of a sudden Bonney told Chisum
To stand up when he expected a beating
But when he stayed seated looking glum

Still Bonney put a pistol in his mouth
When it opened for the fork with steak
And then ordered him with word uncouth
To stand up in his chair or he'd break

Some front teeth but then when he knew
Chisum wasn't hiding a gun Bonney said
Soon after one of the stage coach crew
Ran in the door to say they would head

For Lincoln that Chisum was free to go
Since he isn't worth killing an action
That made Chisum who was normally slow
Run from the room planning retaliation

Doc Scurlock Leaves for Texas

Doc Scurlock had thought about leaving
New Mexico for a long time now because
There was no future in cattle thieving
Which everyone there did without pause

And included friends Bowdre and Bonney
Who almost always had extreme pleasure
In rustling beef like two boys at play
Discovering a chest of pirate treasure

Which was all the more fun when cattle
Belonged to John Chisum who had turned
Away from McSween and would not settle
Debts which as far as he was concerned

Existed only in fantasy and so refused
To pay for services needed for the war
Creating the effect they all felt used
Which left them with a gangrenous scar

Full of poison whose only antidote was
Stealing his cattle off from the range
Showing no respect for any of the laws
Or larger ranchers they might estrange

Joining Dave Rudabaugh and Tom Pickett
Who rode with Billy all of that summer
Since benevolent nature appeared upset
And sent swarms of locust to Ft Sumner

Until dark skies like an ominous cloud
Would descend and soon eat every green
Living leaf that was planted or plowed
Leaving behind famine a desolate scene

A wide corridor of demonic destruction
Where flea infestations came to invade
Men and animals alike and malnutrition
Spread across that land where no shade

Trees were because of the long draught
Which was remarkable for a desert even
Especially if for hours Doc was caught
Out in a violent sun like a bread oven

The reason why he would load the wagon
With belongings and then take his wife
And children and head for a Texas town
That knew far less hardship and strife

Pat Garrett Was Elected Sheriff

When John Chisum learned a new gang of
Rustlers which included William Bonney
Were in Ft Sumner he knew that Sheriff
Kimbrell the Sheriff of Lincoln County

Could be defeated in the next election
By Pat Garrett who Chisum had asked to
Move so he could run for that position
By telling Beaver Smith he was through

Bartending at his saloon where he knew
Bonney and some others liked to gamble
At cards and where he served that crew
Drinks many times as they would ramble

In and out of town on secret escapades
And later on knew Barney Mason so well
He started to snitch against compadres
For the promise of staying out of jail

This long before everyone knew Garrett
Would win the elections by one hundred
And forty one votes and then would let
Mason start to be his informer instead

Since later that year they would marry
Girl friends in a double wedding given
In the town of Anton Chico in the very
Same church using the same priest even

With Bonney and Bowdre out in the pews
Because they helped to put Pat Garrett
Back on his feet after they heard news
The buffalo hunter had come in and met

Hard times because buffalo were scarce
Now a days as they gathered large tips
For that tall bartender who would pace
To and fro on legs so long at the hips

Everyone thought he was wearing stilts
Caring less just as long as Pat cheats
By looking away the second Billy lifts
Blankets off the wagon to reveal meats

Stolen from Chisum herds but meant for
The dispossessed mud dwelling peasants
Hispanic families of Fort Sumners poor
On whom he showered gifts and presents

Agents Track Counterfeit Money
100

Special Agent Azariah Wild was sent by
The US Treasury to look into questions
About counterfeit bills and to ask why
Fake money turned up in all directions

Especially in the hands of James Dolan
Who received a one hundred dollar bill
Illegally given to him by Billy Wilson
Who was cheated and now wanted to kill

The two men who did it Harvey West and
Sam Dedrick who bought a livery stable
From him at White Oaks a frontier kind
Of town where Agent Wild would be able

To begin investigation but whose first
Line of business was to call on lawyer
Ira Leonard who startled his new guest
By showing him William Bonney's letter

Written in his neat hand and then said
Gov Wallace had promised to pardon him
And that he needed lawyer Leonards aid
To approach the Governor since his aim

Was to marry his girl and finally stop
Running from the law an idea that Wild
Supported if he surrendered and on top
Would bear witness to that brain child

He created namely the gang of Rustlers
Who with Bonney had reached White Oaks
Just as Garrett and Mason two hustlers
Located Wild and ultimately shall coax

The Agent into staying put in the town
While Garrett rides alone to Ft Sumner
In the hopes that he shall soon return
With a posse to finish off this matter

While stalling for time he sends Mason
A past gang member to Dedrick's stable
To hear clandestine plans but who soon
Departed when suspicion around a table

Made Bonney say Mason should be killed
Before he informs on their whereabouts
Actions which Dedrick suddenly quelled
Denying that Mason knew their hideouts

The Rustlers Steal Some Groceries

At about noon Bonney went to the house
Of Ira Leonard and knocked on the door
When a housekeeper with a white blouse
Said he went to Lincoln the day before

Which was disappointing news to Bonney
Who hoped the lawyer asked Gov Wallace
About his pardon since he was the only
Outlaw in these parts they could trace

To the morning murder of Sheriff Brady
A pardon that Gov Wallace had promised
But he had delayed some months already
For various reasons that Bonney missed

And believed he had no hope of winning
When he soon mounted his horse instead
To ride the streets of the gold mining
Town of White Oaks knowing in his head

Peppin and Dolan and Matthews had made
Their case in court and were found not
Guilty for crimes that drove Billy mad
Enough to kill all of them on the spot

When he came to the stable and noticed
The boys lugging boxes of canned foods
Into the back room where his eyes iced
Over because they had stolen dry goods

From the general store they walked out
Of without paying a damn foolish thing
Billy said his voice raised in a shout
Because an error like that could bring

Every lawman down right on top of them
Until feeling bad they sobered up some
And came together to solve the problem
By letting friends haul groceries home

In the wagon soon as everyone had left
For their hideout over at Blake's mill
Leaving nine mares from a former theft
Inside Dedricks and Wests stable until

Later on when the gang decided one day
To place horses up for sale at auction
In neighboring towns where farmers pay
Billy sixteen hundred without question

The Rustlers Flee from Ambush

The Kid was right Barney Mason was now
An informant who went to speak to Will
Hudgens the Deputy who had learned how
Through him the stolen stuff was still

In Sam Dedrick's stables waiting to be
Carried to the Rustlers secret hideout
While Mose Dedrick and Lamper would be
Completely oblivious to their stakeout

Also an idea that worked since neither
Soul in the wagon knew they were being
Followed and then continued on further
Past Blake's Mill to unload everything

Before they came back and ran straight
Into the posse that planned the ambush
Then instead of shooting them on sight
Surrounded the wagon to tell them hush

While Hudgens trailed the horse tracks
Left there in fresh falling snow until
He caught the gang unaware with cracks
Of Winchester rifles that quickly kill

Three horses within a running gunfight
So Bonney and Wilson will wander afoot
Through the dark grove in the twilight
Where believe it or not a distant shot

Killed a horse that belonged to Deputy
Hudgens who would not chase after them
Because he thought above all else duty
Demanded he retrieve the missing items

The thieves had carried from his store
Without payment of even a single penny
Hoping they see the gang and once more
Have the opportunity to capture Bonney

Sometime later after they move the two
Prisoners tied up in back of the wagon
So Mose Dedrick can pay a bond in town
Before the Sheriff learned he had gone

Skipped the county fearing a lynch mob
After Lamper received a light sentence
For his accessory role and did not rob
Hudgens store according to his defense

The Rustlers Kill Deputy Carlyle

At dawn a posse surrounded a small Inn
Greathouse forty miles from White Oaks
And it just happened Bonney and Wilson
Were asleep when Dave Rudabaugh chokes

Not over breakfast from Stern the cook
But a message from Deputy Will Hudgens
That asked they surrender and so shook
Rudabaugh he went to grab his two guns

Tripped and then fell in the next room
Startling Bonney who sat up frightened
And then wildly laughed away the gloom
Charging an atmosphere that heightened

Stern's anxiety since he had to go out
To tell Deputy Hudgens the gang wanted
Time to discuss terms of surrender but
Would resist them and remain undaunted

Unless they negotiated first so it was
Deputy Carlyle who volunteered to talk
With the gang who traded Greathouse as
A hostage upon request while the clock

Above the bar wall ticked away an hour
With not a sign of the gangs surrender
While Rudabaugh and Wilson turned sour
At every proposal and just got drunker

Along with Deputy Carlyle who was told
To drink when they filled up his glass
Until ready to fall over he would fold
His head on his arm hoping not to pass

Out on top of the bar when of a sudden
Perhaps around eleven o'clock at night
They heard the voice of Deputy Hudgens
Say unless their eyes soon catch sight

Of Carlyle they would shoot Greathouse
A plan gone mad when they heard a shot
Then without realizing this was a ruse
Carlyle leapt out a window on the spot

And was shot dead by those Rustlers as
A stunned posse left Carlyle all alone
But burnt the house to avenge his loss
Long afterwards when the gang had gone

Pat Garrett Pursues the Rustlers

With a posse of twenty men Pat Garrett
Left his home in Roswell to ride north
Near Bosque Grande Ranch there to meet
Daniel Dedrick and for what it's worth

Seize stolen livestock on his property
Although none were found they did find
After having checked the place a party
Of two escaped prisoners who they bind

By tying their hands with ropes before
Going on to search the Yerby ranch and
See the rider in the distance who wore
A duster and recognize one of the band

Tom O'Folliard thru the telescope lens
And instantly take a short cut to come
Behind him before he warns his friends
But a fresher horse reached their home

Before they can overtake him in battle
And so caution was used when they went
To look in every room and would rattle
Charlie Bowdres wife who suddenly bent

Over double and yelled in a loud voice
For them to get out before her husband
Killed them threats they hardly notice
When the man holding her used his hand

To feel her buttocks before letting go
Which brought a curse down on his ears
And made Garrett and them all laugh so
Hard their faces became wet with tears

When they again went out to the corral
And got two mules and four horses from
Manuela who saw this act being immoral
And with her butcher knife would storm

Outside and stand angrily on the steps
And yell in the way a goose would hiss
You bastards as Billys small dog yelps
And even bites one of the men who piss

In the yard before mounting and riding
Away with some mules and horses in tow
After the elderly woman tried bringing
Her inside in hopes the posse would go

Pat Garrett Takes Prisoners to Jail
105

When Pat Garrett returned to Ft Sumner
Tom Wilcox told him that Bowdre wanted
To meet and talk with him after dinner
And so that next day Garrett sauntered

Upon his horse over to where two forks
Meet in the road where an angry Bowdre
Waits on his horse and suddenly shocks
Garrett who believes that he was there

To surrender and then ask for the bond
But instead insults him when saying in
A dramatic voice the posse went beyond
Limits of the law even committed a sin

By harassing his wife Manuela and that
If Garrett came to the ranch once more
Bowdre would shoot him down like a rat
A serious threat that Pat Garrett bore

With patience and then afterwards said
By feeding the Kid's gang Bowdre would
Risk his family to the hazards of raid
That would come whenever a posse would

Return to capture them perhaps any day
And this was the agreement on the road
When each would depart a different way
So Garrett could get a wagon then load

Dave Rudabaughs pals in wrist manacles
Inside the back then ride to Las Vegas
When five miles traveled like miracles
They see a huge all Mexican posse pass

Coming from Puerto de Luna then return
Wanting a closer look at the prisoners
Webb and Davis whom Garrett will learn
They had hunted for and to cut corners

Agreed to release both prisoners until
Webb becomes afraid of the deadly mood
Of those Mexicans who he believes will
Want to lynch him up from a cottonwood

So pays Garrett ten dollars to stay on
Because it was his duty and so Garrett
Again agreed and asked the posse along
Something he will later come to regret

Pat Garrett Resists Deputy Leyba

As soon as they arrived in the village
Of Puerto de Luna their prisoners were
Taken to a blacksmiths where in a rage
Leyba learned from the prisoners there

That the man with Garrett Barney Mason
Was a member of the Kid's gang and yet
Had no shackles and to know the reason
Leyba immediately went to find Garrett

Who ate at Grzelachowskis roadside inn
With the hungry posse so it was chance
That Garrett came out as Leyba went in
And paused and in a kind of hot trance

Told Garrett he wanted to arrest Mason
Then fired his pistola harmlessly down
At the ground an act that warned Mason
Who then fired a rifle shot of his own

From inside the inn hitting the Deputy
His shoulder before asking if he could
Cut him down like he was made of putty
A cruel and thoughtless act that would

Get Garrett in trouble when the leader
Of the posse a Deputy Francisco Romero
Would disarm then place both men under
Arrest and would wait until the morrow

When he released the two men from jail
After they had explained what happened
In front of a Justice when a cold gale
Blew in from the North and then pinned

Everyone down inside of Gerhardt Ranch
A way station on the road to Las Vegas
Where Garrett will soon act on a hunch
Frank Stewart a cattle agent will pass

By Anton Chico when Garrett would send
Barney Mason there to inform the agent
Who trailed Billy the Kid and his kind
To meet him in Las Vegas where he went

Soon after that posse discovered Mason
Gone and questioned Garrett over lunch
Who said arrest him if they had reason
Then left glad to be rid of that bunch

Stewart Enlists Texas Cowboys

Charlie Siringo sent his Texas cowboys
To Anton Chico while he himself stayed
In Las Vegas to do business and enjoys
Instead gambling halls where he played

The Monte table and lost lots of money
Required to feed and supply his outfit
He being attracted like a bee to honey
Which some cowboys didn't like one bit

When Siringo found them in Anton Chico
Drunk and quarreling with local people
Which drove posse leader Robinson loco
And in the hopes to avoid more trouble

Quickly moved the outfit to White Oaks
Where after a few days they shall meet
With the agent Frank Stewart who talks
Until his face becomes red like a beet

Because Siringo called him a damn liar
When he said five hundred Texas cattle
Were found by Garrett inside of a lair
Since Mason in a characteristic tattle

Had already told Siringo Pat had found
Only seven cattle in Los Portales cave
A place this gang was supposedly bound
After which Stewart would try and save

The day by asking the men to volunteer
In a manhunt which neither Siringo nor
Robinson the two leaders would go near
Because they read in the news Governor

Wallace had made a five hundred dollar
Reward in the arrest of William Bonney
An event that didn't require a scholar
To figure out who got all of the money

Well of course Pat Garrett the Sheriff
The reason why Siringo told Stewart no
They refused to freeze their butts off
For nothing and yet seven agreed to go

Look for the Rustlers around Ft Sumner
Where young Jose Roival went all alone
As a spy and reported to Garrett after
The Kid and his gang were seen in town

Pat Garrett Sets the Death Trap

Early that morning December nineteenth
Eighteen eighty Pat Garrett spied Juan
Gallegos and then went to great length
To talk with that boy in the plaza and

Then ask many questions of him because
He felt certain that the Rustlers were
At Wilcox's ranch and so after a pause
Wilcox's stepson agreed they hid there

And then said he now would do whatever
Was needed since Garretts silver badge
Shining on his vest acted like a lever
For someone so young and tender in age

The naive condition Garrett counted on
When he hurried back to the old Indian
Hospital then sharply spoke when alone
To Jose Valdez upon whom he would lean

With a pistol pointed up at his temple
So he would jot down every single word
Then say Garrett went away for example
To Roswell so everything was in accord

With his plan which if it worked would
Capture the Kid and his gang very soon
So that Valdez sobbed knowing he could
Doubtless sentence his friends to doom

When Garrett using a clean sheet wrote
A second note asking his friend Wilcox
For help and with wax sealed each note
Before setting the candle upon the box

Where the flame flickered like a torch
As soon as a deputy opened up the door
And said the boy waited upon the porch
Juan Gallegos an easily impressed poor

Misguided youth who would later regret
Cooperating so innocently with the law
By agreeing to carry notes for Garrett
The content of which he never even saw

But would on reaching the Wilcox ranch
Deliver to his stepfather plus the Kid
Who having often dealt with that bunch
Should suspect something but never did

Pat Garrett Shoots Tom O'Folliard

Garrett and his men were playing cards
When a guard came in the door and said
Riders were coming a few hundred yards
Distant and so Garrett nodded his head

Quickly rose and blew out a lamp light
Before walking outside of the hospital
His guards had surrounded in the night
And waited on the darkened porch until

The riders would appear along the road
Which a sky with falling snow obscured
While he a Winchester rifle shall load
Getting ready for six victims he lured

Who felt cold and so the horses canter
O'Folliard and Pickett riding in front
And Rudabaugh and Bowdre in the center
While Wilson and Bonney whom they hunt

Take up the rear because Bonney wanted
To ask Wilson for some chewing tobacco
The reason why he turned and sauntered
Just before Garrett's voice would echo

Say raise your hands and a rifle blast
Was heard that tears O'Folliard's guts
So that the surprised gang turned fast
Whirled about on their horses then put

As much space between them as possible
Everyone that is except Tom O'Folliard
Whose skittish mount became unreliable
Until he again got control in the yard

So he could reemerge again in the snow
A couple of minutes later to tell them
Oh please don't shoot me I'm dying now
And in my condition can't be a problem

While embittered Barney Mason screamed
Take your medicine in an act of hatred
As a dazed gang instinctually streamed
Headlong on the road and soon faltered

When Rudabaughs horse fell with wounds
So that he rides doubled behind Wilson
Least to the ranch and there confounds
Wilcox who hurried to hide his stepson

O'Folliard Dies from His Wounds

Garrett suspected a wounded O'Folliard
Could be dangerous when they came near
And so warned Stewarts men in the yard
To disarm this desperado from the rear

Which they did and thinking the outlaw
Still might trick them Pat ordered him
To throw up both hands until Mason saw
From the wounds severity that his time

Was up and was reason he made no moves
Sitting in that saddle perfectly still
His head slumped over a pair of gloves
Which thrashed wildly in the air until

They ceased carrying him and then laid
His outstretched body out on a blanket
Inside of all places where Bowdre paid
Rent for a room that had an old musket

On the wall above the fireplace mantel
In which logs burned until it was nice
And warm there also before they settle
Down and play cards with a set of dice

Since Texas cowboys were not the least
Interested in O'Folliard who they knew
Would be dead soon save for James East
Who would give him water and then show

Him human kindness when those had none
Especially since O'Folliard frequently
Asked Garrett to kill him with his gun
Words that so miffed Mason he suddenly

Interrupted the game of poker to shout
And tell O'Folliard take your medicine
As if though his disease was like gout
Then only provoked O'Folliard to whine

This was the best medicine he ever ate
Until within three quarters of an hour
He died of wounds that sealed his fate
Sometime after he wanted East to scour

His bag for letters to his grandmother
That said I'm coming home to Texas now
With friend Bonney and so don't bother
Worrying it doesn't do any good anyhow

Pat Garrett Follows a Cold Trail

The next day Garrett led his posse out
Along the road maybe expecting to find
More of the Kids gang when lying about
He saw a horse not what he had in mind

Although it belonged to Dave Rudabaugh
Who afterwards sat right behind Wilson
While a posse rode under a heavy bough
The winter being at its coldest season

A hardened ground covered by deep snow
And so returned in awhile to Ft Sumner
Where Tom O'Folliard's burial would go
On in spite of that raw bitter weather

He being put to rest in a plain coffin
With some posse members at his funeral
Like Pat Garrett who afterwards ran in
Shivering to keep warm in the hospital

Around the pot bellied cast iron stove
Where no one realized at those moments
Billy Bonney did not even have a glove
To cover up his hand from the elements

Whose wind howled like the hungry wolf
While they stood guard in anticipation
For Pat Garrett's arrival because self
Preservation decides courses of action

Including this decision to ambush them
If Garrett should appear at the Brazil
And Wilcox Ranch to create more mayhem
After Pickett had separated then still

Found his way there early that morning
To reunite with the gang who grew cold
And weary on the hills with it snowing
So hard even Bonneys spirit would fold

As he agreed to head for the inn where
They ate meals and Wilson assured them
That his stepson took the note unaware
Of the real seriousness of the problem

Or how else could Garrett set the trap
Telling a tale they all felt reluctant
To believe as they read a location map
And then departed there on the instant

Pat Garrett Kills Charlie Bowdre
112

At midnight Pat Garrett heard knocking
On the door and then quickly opened it
Just as Wayne Brazil revealed shocking
News saying that Bonney and his outfit

Left around an hour ago from his ranch
Words that spurred Garrett into action
As he woke the house then with a bunch
Of sleepy riders rode in the direction

Of the ranch where they spotted tracks
In the snow that would lead to a place
Stinking Springs a house made of rocks
And except for this one thing no trace

Of the farm that once tried to scratch
Out some existence here and so Garrett
Knew they were trapped and would hatch
In his brain plans that deserved merit

Leaving all but three men with Stewart
To look after their horses when he and
The other two men would crawl and part
Up an arroyo where Garrett would stand

With a rifle twenty feet from the door
That opened in the house in the center
After they heard those occupants snore
Then laid on blankets but do not enter

To wait for that sun to rise of course
When the man Charlie Bowdre with a hat
Like a sombrero walked up to his horse
With a feed bag as a shot would impact

Him from Garrett's gun without warning
Twice in the chest and once in the leg
By others when Bowdre backward falling
Leaned up against Bonney who would beg

His friend to kill the sons of bitches
Before he died and turned his gun belt
So that it faced on his front britches
And then urged him out where none felt

At risk when Bowdre hands raised slips
In the snow to land on his back beside
Lee Hall and said from his bloody lips
These last words I wish before he died

Capture at Stinking Springs
113   Part I

Suddenly Bonney reached a hand through
The doorway where the horses were tied
By ropes to the rafter and even though
He had safely pulled two horses inside

Louis Bousman shot a third in the neck
Dropped it in an instant its shoulders
In the doorway so they could not break
Out from there past Garrett and others

Who with a rifle made a marksmans shot
Cut the rope into and freed the horses
Who whinnied then ran off to be caught
Later on by certain men with the posse

When Bousman followed Garretts example
And fired rifles at stones in the wall
Hoping the horses inside would trample
Billy and stop him from leaving at all

On a wolf dart he learned from Indians
By riding to one side shooting his gun
But stopped afraid if his horse stands
He would his head on that doorway stun

This just minutes before a chuck wagon
Came with Wilcox the driver his breath
Having frozen his beard as his stepson
Fearing someone would be shot to death

Wasted no time in building the bonfire
At around three and then cooked a meal
Of bacon Bonney would smell and desire
So much he would make an offer or deal

To Pat Garrett by their waving a white
Handkerchief out the chimney signaling
A temporary truce that Rudabaugh might
Negotiate terms and does by requesting

Jail at Santa Fe because a Mexican mob
Would hang him at Las Vegas for things
He had done there during his brief job
As Deputy so Garrett agrees and brings

The situation to a close after telling
The gang to leave their weapons behind
In the house and come forward throwing
Up their hands like leaves in the wind

Capture at Stinking Springs
114   Part II

When Bonney met the Deputies who stood
On the knoll he came up to shake hands
With everyone but Mason who understood
Why when Bonney upset and angry brands

Him the worst kind of traitor unawares
Mason would level a gun at him as soon
As he had walked on by until he stares
Looking back and in surprise saw Mason

Being covered with rifles belonging to
East and Hall who told Barney to carry
Bowdre over to the wagon and be pronto
Since everyone was cold and in a hurry

To reach Ft Sumner with four prisoners
Who rode on horses part of the way and
Then in the wagon right by this goners
Frozen corpse until they came to stand

Before the smithy who welded leg irons
Around the men's ankles before Garrett
Kept his promise at one of the saloons
Beaver Smiths where he used to work at

And let them take their pick from menu
Because the county paid for every part
Since it was there Bonney gave his new
Rifle to East and then offered Stewart

Only temporary loan of a fine bay mare
Which otherwise would have no exercise
When East told them what happened here
Only minutes ago what was the surprise

Of his life as he carried Bowdres body
Across the door of the small apartment
When they spied Manuela who felt moody
And spoke in Spanish words which meant

They were damn rotten bastards and hit
The top of his head with what Tom Hill
Believed looked like a stove poker but
Was actually a branding iron and still

Hurt since the woman was driven insane
And her blows made him drop the corpse
At her feet and then run from the pain
She swearing that whole time of course

The New Celebrities of Las Vegas

They left Ft Sumner early the next day
All four prisoners riding in the wagon
Which gave Bonney only a moment to say
A few words in the first blush of dawn

To Deluvina Maxwell the adopted Navajo
Woman he spoke to with great affection
And then called his mother even though
She wailed because he was in detention

But that hardly bothered Bonney at all
Who felt high spirited during the trip
Along with Dave Rudabaugh who was tall
And rotund and would often sneer a lip

Or crack a joke to cheer the day along
Until at Puerto de Luna they soon meet
At Gazelachowskis Road House for among
Other things Christmas dinner then eat

Everything on that menu since it might
Be their last good meal at least until
They arrived in Las Vegas within sight
Of a large crowd who seemed to delight

At seeing Billy the Kid who smiled and
Waved at folks like a famous celebrity
Yet spit at Rudabaugh who they planned
To lynch as soon as they lost sobriety

Because they resented Dave for killing
Lino Valdez an unfortunate man he hung
From the town's windmill after telling
Rudabaugh he was part of a wanted gang

And for this reason shouted complaints
Until he was locked up behind bars and
Was given a brand new suit compliments
Of mail contractors who took the stand

Publicity would bring in more business
And so had them all looking their best
On the day Bonney reports to the Press
To the Las Vegas Optic that the latest

Tally of those who died in the Lincoln
County War was over two hundred but he
Did not kill them all and had acted in
Self defense and so should pardoned be

An Angry Mob Stops the Train

One day the prisoners who were chained
Together were suddenly switched around
Since Deputy Romero of Las Vegas aimed
To hold one pair until they were bound

Over for trial even though Pat Garrett
Protested and he would eventually halt
Further confinement when Frank Stewart
Signed affidavits that expressed fault

Until the frightened Deputy unfettered
Rudabaugh who robbed a federal carrier
Of mail something the Deputy regretted
When Romero said becoming even angrier

Garrett was a damn liar if he knew one
Then raced down to the station as fast
As both legs could run taking everyone
Along with him who remembered the past

Misdeeds of Rudabaugh who had murdered
The jailor in an escape and who was so
Afraid of being stopped and surrounded
Garrett became uncertain of what to do

Except guard the car door with a rifle
As Frank Stewart protected the far end
Hoping at any minute to hear a whistle
Before Romero found the time to ascend

A platform in front of the angry crowd
Made of Mexican villagers and settlers
To retake Rudabaugh until he was cowed
By Garrett who like an elk its antlers

Shake to scare away the pack of wolves
Now shakes his rifle and swears to arm
The gang so they can defend themselves
If that mob showed signs of doing harm

Saying it in a voice as calm as can be
Until he convinced Romero to step down
Clear the platform so Inspector Morley
Can make certain the train leaves town

By freeing engineers taken as hostages
Before the locomotive runs along rails
Very much like a fiery beast and rages
From a steam whistle that loudly wails

The Court Reopens in the Spring

Once they arrived at the Santa Fe jail
The prisoners went immediately to work
After realizing none could afford bail
To dig a tunnel which the prison clerk

Discovered one day after seeing a pile
Of dirt neatly hidden under mattresses
And seeing they would escape in awhile
Decided to become one of the witnesses

Who quickly made Sheriff Martinez wary
So that Martinez immediately separated
Bonney and locked him away in solitary
Where for weeks no sunlight penetrated

And no news was heard from the outside
Until one day the attorney Ira Leonard
Came to stand at the table by his side
To whisper they must go rapidly onward

Because Rudabaugh had gotten convicted
On three counts of mail theft and then
Taken to Las Vegas where Ira predicted
Dave would stand trial for murder when

The court reopened for the spring term
News that didn't really startle Bonney
Who decided to hire Leonard's law firm
Then pay for expensive fees with money

Gotten if someone sold his prized mare
So that when spring court got underway
Ira Leonard came from White Oaks there
To appear inside of the house each day

To defend Bonney on charges of killing
Buckshot Roberts which ultimately were
Dismissed after Ira Leonards thrilling
Discovery Judge Bristol wanted to blur

A fine technical point of the law when
Admitting federal indictments in court
Without considering Blazers Mills then
As now was private land and must abort

The trial in order to turn Bonney over
To the territorial authorities instead
Which everyone thought was very clever
And gave Bonney the hope to look ahead

Bonney Was Sentenced to Hang

Many people wanted to see Bonney tried
For the murder of Sheriff Brady and so
The hot and crowded room showed a wide
Mix of Indians and peoples from Mexico

And from Europe who vied for a glimpse
Of the now famous outlaw Billy the Kid
Who sat at table next to legal defense
Attorney Albert Fountain who would bid

The court to dismiss charges of murder
On grounds of self defense but Bristol
The Judge refused to hear this further
Instead heard people say with a pistol

Bonney had shot and killed the Sheriff
With at least half a dozen said gunman
Who hid behind the store for one brief
Moment before killing him and Hindmann

In what became very damaging testimony
From some of Billys most hated enemies
Like James Dolan who made enough money
To appeal conviction a number of times

Not to mention men like Sheriff Peppin
And Deputy Matthews whose good friends
In the rich and powerful Santa Fe Ring
Often applied different ways and means

Than Bonney who pleaded in his letters
To Wallace saying he had done all that
He was asked but that in these matters
The Governor had failed to do all what

He had promised before he had resigned
Then left no pardon or signed document
To rescue his name from being maligned
By the newspapers so that the judgment

Found by this jury declared him guilty
Of murder then heard his sentence read
To them by Judge Bristol who brutishly
Wished him hung by the neck until dead

This punishment carried out in Lincoln
Within thirty days while Bonney stared
At the Judge without emotion just then
When he had realized that nobody cared

Bonney Was Escorted to Lincoln

Next day Bonney was chained to a wagon
Seat and then squeezed in between John
McKinney whose scar still had not gone
From a cheek Bonney wounded with a gun

Plus Billy Matthews a Deputy he fought
In the Lincoln battle when across from
Him Bob Olinger buried in deep thought
Now spoke to tell everyone how he came

To kill John Jones that day at Pierces
Ranch where Jones came to turn himself
In for cutting John Beckwith to pieces
In a fight for stolen cattle that left

Olinger mad for revenge since Beckwith
Had been his friend a false story that
Rankled Bonney making him explode with
Anger since he knew for matter of fact

Olinger had killed John Jones shooting
Him in the back while Milo Pierce held
His hand in a handshake he not letting
Go of that hand until Jones was felled

By a bullet from the executioner's gun
Wounding Milo in the thigh and forever
Crippling him in words that would stun
Olinger who of a sudden sprang panther

Like to sink his hands over the throat
Of the Kid and then choke him to death
And would have but for that thick coat
The Kid had on as he caught his breath

Gasping for air after the others throw
Olinger off and quickly make the wagon
Halt since Olinger hated Bonney anyhow
And could ride his horse to Ft Stanton

Where Pat Garrett was waiting for them
And where Billy was allowed to stretch
His legs and exercise before seven men
Everyone with knowledge he would fetch

Garrett a high reward for catching him
Everyone afraid of his most deadly gun
When compared to Garrett tall and grim
Yet liked Bonney who was short and fun

Bob Olinger Tries to Bully Bonney

Beginning that day Olinger would bully
Bonney whenever he had the opportunity
Example when Ella Bolton visited Billy
On Sunday seeing it her religious duty

To bring him some molasses cookies she
Knew he liked and then instantly hated
It because he would hang from the tree
Leaving her so helpless and frustrated

But surprised too since he would smile
Like a mischievous boy of endless hope
Saying that he planned on being a mile
Away on May thirteenth that day a rope

Had been scheduled to stretch his neck
And added with a laugh if I'm not here
They can't hang me so that she'd check
For a lace handkerchief to wipe a tear

In the same instant Olinger heard what
The Kid had said and then became blind
With rage and put his gun up like that
As if to club him but made up his mind

Not to do it with the lady in the room
Located on the second floor of the old
Dolan store that had seen lots of doom
Years before Thomas Catron had it sold

To cancel a debt he owed in back taxes
So the town had a new place for a jail
Where Bonney in shackles never relaxes
As each day grows profitless and stale

Yet constantly hopes that some friends
Will come there to engineer his escape
And now whispers to achieve these ends
Saying he'd gotten a pretty bad scrape

But expected freedom before that event
And this overheard angered Bob Olinger
So much he would explode and then vent
Hatred on the Kid as Ella would linger

Suddenly riveted and deeply enthralled
When Bob Olinger would threaten Bonney
Telling him that if his friends called
He would die before they found the key

Bonney Recalls Stepfather Antrim

Bonney had experienced problems before
Catherine McCarty a loving good mother
Died of tuberculosis and left two poor
Orphans at mercy of a cruel stepfather

William Antrim who soon left to strike
Riches in Arizona he having had enough
Of Silver City and boys he didn't like
Since his character was cold and gruff

And he was a drunkard who quickly left
Billy and older brother Joe in care of
The Truesdells after being made bereft
By his young wife Catherine whose love

For people placed her in good standing
At the Star Hotel where she had worked
Before so that Billy got a job waiting
On tables and then broke into a locked

Laundry to steal from Chinaman Charlie
Two hundred dollars besides taking two
Guns and some suit clothes which Billy
Stored in his room to keep off the dew

Until he and Sombrero Jack could split
Up the chest of treasure or would have
Before Sarah Brown looked and found it
While cleaning out the closet and gave

Away their secret to Sheriff Whitehill
Who locked these boys behind iron bars
To scare and teach them a lesson until
They escaped and he sounded the alarms

When a jailor discovered they had gone
By climbing right up through a chimney
To the big surprise of nearly everyone
In the town who had thought this funny

Especially old men who told this story
Over and over again to wonder what new
Thing the town could expect from Henry
Who became invisible and suddenly blew

Into Arizona to look up his stepfather
Who in a drunken rage burned the house
Out of spite when they fought together
So Henry would fly on a borrowed horse

Kid Antrim Shoots Windy Cahill

Afterwards Kid Antrim hired on to work
A cheese farm down upon the Gila River
Beside Charlie Bowdre and Doc Scurlock
Two men who became his friends forever

Until one day as they sat eating lunch
Those uneasy wranglers decided to move
To become business partners in a ranch
In Lincoln County with wives they love

Because Lincoln became the county seat
And so when they left he stayed behind
Near Ft Grant where he would soon meet
Others cut from cloth of the same kind

Like ex soldier John Mackie the leader
Of a gang who gathered for the purpose
Of rustling horses the sort of plunder
The Kid aspired to reach in due course

Being fired from Hooker's cattle ranch
Since a cowboys life was too difficult
And he got more money at serving lunch
In the saloon for Miles a mature adult

Who astonished both he and Mackie with
A pistol hidden behind a waiter's tray
And then forced them to walk the width
Of two miles since it was how far away

Ft Grant was seated from Hotel De Luna
Where Henry had worked as a waiter too
Till free on bond he visited a cantina
Where Windy Cahill sat at the barstool

The blacksmith who fitted his shackles
A big arrogant bully who called Antrim
A pimp and lover boy just for chuckles
Before Antrim exchanged words with him

Until Cahill lifted him like a feather
And threw him down to pin his shoulder
Began to choke him and he drew leather
Pulled his pistol and shot the soldier

Wounding him in the gut so that Cahill
Lived for three days being very ornery
And in an affidavit said he was killed
For nothing and blamed it all on Henry

Billy the Kid Shoots James W Bell

Bonney needed help if he was to escape
From where he was confined by shackles
Inside the room that like a death trap
Bound him so neither force of knuckles

Nor strain could loosen from the floor
The bolted iron chains until gradually
Bonney grew sick and had diarrhea more
Often than human beings have generally

So that for Deputy Bell it was routine
To free him from the bondage of chains
And walk him downstairs to the latrine
To guard the prisoner with great pains

He still unaware that Bonney had eaten
Jalapenos and that they were the cause
Of his discomfort until once too often
Bonney would read newspapers and pause

Inside the outhouse with a door closed
For reasons of privacy and then return
Back up the courthouse stairs composed
And confident where soon he would turn

Round and then face Bell with a pistol
Gripped in his right hand and then ask
Bell to lay down his gun and not stall
For time but concentrate upon the task

Of taking the manacles from his wrists
With the key that hung on the far wall
That Bell did do with calculated risks
Before like a fool he ignored the yell

From Bonney and then ran straight over
To descend the stairs when Bonney shot
Bell right in the back with a revolver
Causing him to run and lie on the spot

Where he fell just inside the backyard
A few yards from Godfrey Gauss who had
Heard the gunshot and then run forward
To check on Bell's pulse with his hand

And now instantly realized he was dead
That Billy the Kid had shot the Deputy
Bringing his dramatic escape to a head
When Pat Garrett had gone away on duty

Billy the Kid Shoots Bob Olinger

Five minutes earlier Olinger had taken
Several petty criminals to the Wortley
For dinner where the shot would awaken
An alarm in the hotel and then shortly

Compel Olinger to run instantly across
Main Street to stop at the eastern end
Of that courthouse where Godfrey Gauss
An accomplice who was a janitor warned

Olinger the shooting happened upstairs
Bell was dead an event that frightened
The tough Deputy who had been unawares
Until then and further got enlightened

On the instant he heard the Kids voice
Say hello Bob in a second story window
Where he would look up and then notice
His double barrel shotgun directed now

At him about one second before a blast
Of buckshot sprayed his chest and face
So that he fell or collapsed very fast
As if he planned to win hell in a race

That saw Billy the Kid break the stock
Of Olingers shotgun on the window sill
And then throw it on the body to shock
The townspeople who were looking still

And then told his friend Godfrey Gauss
When they had both worked for Tunstall
To quickly bring him Billy Berts horse
That he saw corralled beside the stall

While he ducked inside to pry the link
Loose in his shackle with a metal file
Taken from a tool box next to the sink
As Gauss held onto the horse meanwhile

And waited for Billy the Kid to appear
In fifteen minutes and instantly mount
Only to have the fine black horse rear
Backwards then buck him off on account

Of the shackles loose chains scared it
So that Billy would dust off his pants
By hitting them two times with his hat
Holding his gun in a bow legged stance

Billy the Kid Makes His Escape

Swinging round Billy gazed over toward
A bystander on Main Street a reluctant
Cowboy who he convinced to run forward
To bring back Berts horse this instant

Or else get shot and so watched him go
Catch the fine black mare as the crowd
Stood in silence all men he would know
Who at a different time had been proud

Of what he had done in the Lincoln War
By fighting against the cold injustice
Of powerful men who controlled the law
In town and wound up with murder twice

Tunstall and McSween events remembered
Clearly like it had happened yesterday
So different from when he unencumbered
Dressed in loose fitting clothes today

A borrowed sweater or a pair of gloves
A vest instead of a black suit and tie
Running from the law that no one loves
Since he believed he must fight or die

And protect his friends the exact same
Thing shared by everyone there as well
Who stared and tried hard not to blame
Billy the Kid for shooting Deputy Bell

Because they understood he killed Bell
Not out of malice or spite but because
He had to stop him so he wouldn't tell
Bob Olinger and thereby end that cause

Which many people now openly supported
By telling Billy they hoped he escaped
Something they easily could've aborted
But watched him instead when he draped

His legs in the saddle and swung a gun
In the crowds direction never trusting
Them for a minute as he started to run
The horse at top speed after thrusting

Chains in his boots and spurred flanks
This time not fearing the horse reared
Between two houses built out of planks
A spot last seen before he disappeared

Pat Garrett Hurries for Lincoln

Pat Garrett was attending a meeting in
The town of White Oaks due to an award
Collected by a Cattlemen's Association
Currently represented by Frank Stewart

After Wallace's term as Governor ended
To the great disappointment of Garrett
With no funds to pay some five hundred
Dollars the amount for Bonney's arrest

And conviction when he was interrupted
Half way in his speech by a bald clerk
With a visor cap who quickly disrupted
That meeting having come from his work

At the telegraph office with a message
Saying that William Bonney had escaped
After shooting two deputies an outrage
Which confused Pat Garrett as he gaped

At the audience and read them the news
And then quickly adjourned the meeting
To turn back home with no time to lose
When at Lincoln he received a greeting

With his normal stoicism from citizens
Who would describe the event in detail
As if they looked in a magnifying lens
To tell him how Bonney broke from jail

Blaming Deputy Bell for being friendly
With Billy whose innate cleverness had
Tricked him into something very deadly
Then made the Sheriffs office look bad

Afterwards when he rode off unmolested
While the townspeople had done nothing
So that an escape had gone uncontested
Making Garrett believe that this thing

Was done from fear instead out of pity
By men like Fred Gauss who would crack
Up every time Garrett shirked his duty
Saying the Kid was impossible to track

He having gone to Mexico if he was him
Because he knew of Billy the Kid alias
William H Bonney then alias Kid Antrim
And compared to him Garrett was an ass

Billy the Kid Heads for Ft Sumner

Henry Farmer used to haul freight with
Teams of oxen for John Tunstalls store
And so that day of April twenty eighth
As Henry and two sons worked the chore

Of watering a field planted with wheat
Where Bonito that irrigation river ran
Billy the Kid now withered in the heat
Stopped his horse by a ditch there and

Said howdy to Henry who is quiet until
He looked up and said hello Billy what
You doing here and Billy said I killed
Two Deputies in town breaking free but

I'm going and I doubt if you will ever
See me again a confession that stunned
His two sons who knew this would sever
Friendships when the oldest boy funned

Asked Billy to come down and then play
While Billy didn't have time of course
So appropriately replied I'm on my way
And then kicked the sides of his horse

To ride as fast as the animal could go
For purple mountains that were distant
Hoping nobody would follow him or know
That region he had gone on the instant

He reached Yginio Salazars small shack
Near Las Tablas where Yginio felt glad
To see him and sawed into the shackles
Then did more things to assist the lad

Who had risked his life during the war
For Hispanics who died without remorse
To defend their rights year after year
That included giving him a fresh horse

And making sure that Bert's got placed
Back in the corral doing this secretly
Of course after Billy rested and raced
Toward Fort Sumner where he discretely

Stayed on the outskirts of the village
With shepherds who went back and forth
Crisscrossing a range dotted with sage
Carrying messages from house to hearth

Billy the Kid Meets Abrana Garcia

One shepherd in particular a friend of
Bonneys who shall be named Chico Lopez
Drove to Ft Sumner to pick up his love
A beautiful senorita who everyone says

Was named Abrana Garcia the one Bonney
Had married some months before and who
Would reunite with him for their honey
Moon and bring along his small dog too

Which he named Chico after the name of
His friend who he saw coming in a cart
Which had two very tall wheels made of
Cedar that was being pulled by a smart

Donkey who was short and had long ears
And so Bonney went out to greet Abrana
Who stood up then abandoning all fears
Leaped in his arms like at the cantina

Where they would meet during the dance
Just when the dog grew jealous of them
And then barked so Bonney would glance
Around sideways and then play with him

At their old game of catching the lead
Bullets that Bonney shot into the sand
Like this was the food on which it fed
Before coming to lick the masters hand

At the same time bringing this comment
From Chico Lopez who believed the idea
Of naming a dog Chico sort of indecent
But spoke not a word because of Abrana

Even if he had nobody would have heard
Since right then the couple would kiss
And seeing what came next the shepherd
Withdrew to leave this couple in bliss

As they walked hand in hand to the hut
Then disappeared inside of the bedroom
To undress and check the door was shut
Before doing what each bride and groom

In the world does in love and marriage
Before falling asleep on their pillows
After a very long ride in the carriage
To consummate the blessed wedding vows

Billy the Kids Last Day at Home

While Bonney was lying in bed he heard
Chico in the yard with his donkey cart
And so he got up without saying a word
To Abrana who woke with a sudden start

When he went out the door to see Chico
Who gave him a lovely brace of rabbits
Which he hunted for his favorite amigo
And because women cooked out of habits

Abrana dressed in a short sleeved gown
That showed the outline of her breasts
Took the rabbits as Chico stepped down
Saying she'd prepare one of her feasts

Then cooked the meal as the men talked
Finally serving the table with chilies
And onions which Chico hungrily forked
Down having one of the biggest bellies

While Abrana who was never the shy one
Told Chico she and Billy had conceived
A child last night and hoped for a son
Though neither of the men had believed

That she a woman could know this thing
And wisely let it pass without comment
Since neither man wanted this to bring
About the seeds for a foolish argument

When Chico proposed they drink a toast
Then filled their glasses with tequila
And from much drink made a silly boast
Lowering him to the level of a gorilla

So that words slipped out of his mouth
Letting Abrana know their small secret
That he would take Billy farther south
In his cart to Ft Sumner and so regret

What he had said about Paulita Maxwell
When Abrana quickly showing the temper
Of Spanish blood condemned him to hell
When she stood up and made him scamper

Out of the way because she was jealous
Of another woman no matter what reason
Then shut the door calling him a louse
And Billy a liar to show them a lesson

Billy the Kids Unfinished Business

Without waking his wife Abrana who lay
On the bed so peacefully asleep Bonney
Lingered a part of him wanting to stay
With her but got ready for the journey

By slipping into the shepherds clothes
All white pants and straw sombrero hat
Given to him by Chico and his brothers
Before he walked out to the small cart

And climbed near his apologetic friend
Who drove him all the way to Ft Sumner
Because with firm purpose he would end
The life of Jose Valdez after a manner

Befitting a cowardly traitor who wrote
The letter of lies that had encouraged
All the gang to rendezvous at the spot
Where Garrett was and feeling outraged

Knocked on the door where he had heard
Valdez now lived but found no one home
And so waited inside the peach orchard
Hoping within the hour Jose would come

All the while not seeing two strangers
Who spied on him from the deep shadows
Of the orchard when he quickly hungers
To see Deluvina Maxwell in the windows

The reason he hurried away and knocked
On the door and waited for some answer
When she unlocked it and almost choked
She wearing the cross he had given her

Since her boy was here to see that old
Red skinned Navajo woman who was taken
By Apache and turned into a slave sold
To Lucian Maxwell for only nine broken

Swayed back ponies since he had wanted
Someone to care and nurse his children
When his wife passed and he had hunted
For a new wife but never married again

Who Billy called mother too ever since
She cooked meals and he was now bidden
To butcher a beef quarter near a fence
Outside still unaware of danger hidden

John Poe Arrives on the Scene

John Poe was a detective for the Texas
Cattlemen Association hired to replace
Frank Stewart who had no leads whereas
Mr Poe knew of a tramp who could trace

The exact whereabouts of Billy the Kid
If the lawman gave him a gift of money
Because the man overheard where he hid
While resting in the hayloft as Bonney

Visited a livery stables at White Oaks
Late one night asking for Barney Mason
That traitorous wretched dog who barks
Or befriends Pat Garrett for no reason

And so Poe then paid this homeless man
Not much money but enough to get drunk
After he made the detective understand
The Kid was at Ft Sumner a lot of bunk

According to Pat Garrett when Poe told
Him in Lincoln what the tramp had said
And though at this time he wasn't sold
On the idea he agreed to go if Poe led

The way by going all alone to the town
While they stayed behind in sand dunes
Because Garrett and McKinney are known
To residents there who will play tunes

All different ones for Poe who manages
To question several locals at a saloon
Without arousing suspicion as he wages
They over do it and at the table swoon

Because he could match drink for drink
By pouring his whiskey into a spittoon
Reeking of tobacco juice so they think
That he must be drunk too when he soon

Leaves there without answers then goes
Beyond the town to stay at a ranch run
By Rudolph a friend of Garrett's whose
Edge shows he's afraid of Bonney's gun

And so Poe leaves there early and goes
To meet Garrett at a prearranged place
They reach simultaneously making Poe's
Friends believe he was guided by grace

Pat Garrett Kills Billy the Kid
132   Part I

Then under cover of darkness the three
Men sneak into Ft Sumner and then wait
Two hours in shadows from a peach tree
With a full moon and since it was late

Poe suggests they talk to Pete Maxwell
Who owns the place and so Garrett went
Down orchard paths to stop in and tell
Maxwell news of the Kid while Poe bent

Down then sat on the porch as McKinney
Sat on the white fence near the street
Just inside the gate when Billy Bonney
Suddenly appeared no shirt in the heat

Walking briskly beside the fence as he
Buckled his holster and then surprised
Removed a gun as though stung by a bee
It was that fast after he had realized

Strangers were there then said to them
Quien es Quien es who is it in Spanish
And Poe not revealing any names to him
Thinking the boy a shepherd would wish

He felt no alarm and even said as much
When the Kid walked backwards pointing
His gun now and then stood in a crouch
Behind a thick adobe wall still asking

Quien es some five times in all before
He quickly turned and then disappeared
Inside the bedroom then said once more
Loudly this time to Pete when appeared

A flash a sudden blast from the muzzle
Garretts from where he sat at the head
Of the bed where Bonney leaned puzzled
One moment before he felt burning lead

And moaned his heart with deaths wound
Instantly making him fall to the floor
Where he laid still then without sound
So that Garrett could run out the door

Then brush up against Poe who stood by
The wall where by Garrett came to rest
Then very curiously heard John Poe say
You shot the wrong man this is a guest

Pat Garrett Kills Billy the Kid
Part II

But Garrett insisted he had recognized
Bonneys voice when shadows on his left
Revealed Maxwell who became hypnotized
As Poe about shot him or would have if

Garrett had not acted quickly to knock
Down his hand holding the gun and said
Don't shoot Maxwell who now would balk
When Garrett told him the Kid was dead

At the idea of going into his father's
House to fetch a candle made of tallow
But he did go and walk in his sister's
Room and then return to see the fellow

Garrett had killed by setting a candle
Upon the windowsill so they could look
Inside the dark room at the gun handle
Of ivory and butcher knife but it took

Garrett one moment to realize the body
Which lay with its back upon the floor
Indeed was Billy Bonney before anybody
Was allowed to enter that bedroom door

Where they hid from folks with a light
While news quickly spread that Garrett
Murdered Bonney and may put up a fight
Even more reason why Garrett would let

Neighbors gather but not least at once
Carry his body into a carpenter's shop
Where they laid Bonney on a work bench
Then set candles all around it in hope

Of saving his soul after a night vigil
Since they believed in the forgiveness
Of God and continued the prayers until
That next afternoon when a church mass

Was said for him and every one in town
Attended a funeral at the old cemetery
When four pallbearers lowered him down
In a grave that would be his sanctuary

A resting place alongside good friends
Both Charlie Bowdre and Tom O'Folliard
Where this whole tragic story now ends
But for mourners lingering in the yard

THE END

APPENDIX

The Killers of John Tunstall

Deputy George Hindmann, William 'Buck' Morton, Frank Baker, Bob Beckwith, Dutch Charlie Kruling, Manuel 'Indian' Segovia, Jessie Evans, Tom Hill, and many others.

Members Of The Regulators

Alexander McSween, Dick Brewer, Frank MacNab, Josiah 'Doc' Scurlock, William H Bonney – alias Billy the Kid alias Henry 'Kid' Antrim, Charlie Bowdre, Tom O'Folliard, George and Frank Coe (brothers), Ab Saunders (cousin to the Coes), Fred Waite, Henry Brown, John Middleton, 'Big Jim' French, Jose Chavez, Martin Cheves, Yginio Salazar, Antanacio Martinez, and many others.

The Assassins Of Sheriff Brady

William H Bonney, Fred Waite, John Middleton, Henry Brown, 'Big Jim' French, and Frank MacNab.

Supporters of The House

Lawrence G Murphy, Emil Fritz, James J Dolan, John Riley, Thomas Catron, Col Nathan Dudley, Sheriff William Brady, Deputy George Hindmann, Sheriff George Peppin, Deputy Billy Matthews, Deputy James Longwell, Deputy Buck Powell, Deputy Bob Beckwith, William McCloskey, Buckshot Rogers, and many others.

APPENDIX
153
The Jessie Evans Gang

Jessie Evans, Frank Baker, William 'Buck' Morton, Dolly Graham, Tom Hill, Dick Lloyd, Jimmy McDaniels, Manuel 'Indian' Segovia, Billy Campbell, Andy Boyle, and many others.

The John Kinny Gang

John Kinney, Jim Wallace, R L Bryan, John Chambers, Caleb Hall, Edward Hart, James Hurley, John Irving, George Rose, and many others.

NOTES

William Henry Bonney - Born: November 23, 1859 - Died: July 14, 1881.

Patrick Garrett - Born: June 5, 1850 – Died: February 29, 1908.

Garrett was killed by Wayne Brazil in a dispute over a lease for land and goats. Brazil was charged with murder, but was acquitted after claiming self-defense. Garrett was no longer Sheriff at the time.

BIBLIOGRAPHY

Books

Burns, Walter. *Saga Of Billy The Kid*. Garden City, NY: Double Day, Page & Company, 1926

Coe George. *Frontier Fighter*. Boston and New York: Houghton Mifflin Company. The Riverside Press Cambridge, 1934

Garrett, Pat. *The Life Of Billy The Kid*. New York, NY: Nordon Publications, Inc., (No Year Given).

Klasner, Lily. *My Girlhood Among Outlaws*. Tucson AZ: The University Of Arizona Press, 1972

Utley, Robert. *Billy The Kid: A Short And Violent Life*. Lincoln, NE: University Of Nebraska Press, 1989

Websites

Library of Congress: *American Life Histories: Manuscripts from the Federal Writers Project*, 1936-1940 LOC.Gov

Maxwell, Lucien. *The Maxwell (Beaubien-Miranda) Land Grant and Colfax County War*. Sangres.Com

McCarty, Nick. *Billy the Kid: Outlaw Legend*: Angelfire.Com

Poe, John W. *Death of Billy the Kid*. Article taken from True West Magazine, June 1962 Angelfire.Com/nm/boybanditking/oldfortsumner

Speer, Lucas. *Lucas Speer's Billy the Kid Website*: Angelfire.Com.

Pictures

To see old photographs of many of the people contained within these pages, please take a moment to visit these and other websites by keying in Billy the Kid.

www.ingramcontent.com/pod-product-compliance
Lightning Source LLC
Chambersburg PA
CBHW071724090426
42738CB00009B/1871